MW00423961

Divorce
in Virginia

*The Legal Process,
Your Rights, and What to Expect*

Steven L. Raynor, J.D.

Addicus Books
Omaha, Nebraska

An Addicus Nonfiction Book

ISBN 978-1-938803-88-8
Typography Jack Kusler

This book is not intended to serve as a substitute for an attorney. Nor is it the author's intent to give legal advice contrary to that of an attorney. The information contained in this book is for general informational purposes only and should not be relied upon or considered legal advice applicable to a specific legal matter.

Library of Congress Cataloging-in-Publication Data

Raynor, Steven L., 1960—author.
  Divorce in virginia : understandable answers to your legal questions / Steven L. Raynor, J.D.
        pages cm
  Includes bibliographical references and index.
  ISBN 978-1-938803-88-8 (alk. paper)
  1. Divorce—Law and legislation—Virginia. I. Title.
  KFV2500.R39 2014
  346.75501'66—dc23

                                                    2014016267

Addicus Books, Inc.
P.O. Box 45327
Omaha, Nebraska 68145
www.AddicusBooks.com

Printed in the United States of America
10 9 8 7 6 5 4 3 2

A divorce has rules and procedures.
Learn them.
Knowledge is empowering.

Contents

Acknowledgments

I gratefully acknowledge the attorneys and staff in my office, Kyle Farmer, Jordan Hays, Katie Fisher, Mariel Maughan, and Jamie Wilson, all of whom have assisted in one way or another with this book. I give a special thanks to my publishers Rod Colvin and Jack Kusler, along with editor Gerry Madigan for their help and support in the preparation of this work.

Introduction

Students of history know that our culture and time are unusual in basing marriage on the concepts of a fair, polite, mutually respectful, monogamous, loving, intimate, power-sharing relationship. These lofty ideals often yield relationships that are highly satisfactory to the spouses, but as a result of common human shortcomings they also yield a disappointingly high number of divorces.

Each divorce case is unique, with its own issues, time frame, and dynamics. A person facing a divorce is likely to feel overwhelmed by all of the issues. And the demands of the divorce process come at a time when people are typically stressed and emotional due to all of the life changes associated with the breakdown of the marriage.

No one wants to have to go through a divorce. If you find yourself in that situation, you and your family will benefit if you become educated about the process, the issues, and the law, and if you pursue your divorce in a thoughtful manner. I hope this book assists in that process.

In the context of a divorce, knowledge can help reduce your anxiety and uncertainty, help you avoid costly mistakes, and help you reach a better outcome for you and your children. The knowledge you gain from this book may also reduce your legal costs as your divorce attorney will have to spend less time meeting and discussing with you the process, procedures, and substantive information you will learn from this book.

A divorce case is likely the most important and complicated legal matter you will ever encounter. You need a divorce attorney. This book will provide answers to your general questions, but it is not a substitute for an attorney. Your divorce attorney will be able to give you specific legal advice tailored to the facts of your case and the practices and procedures of your locality.

Steve Raynor
Raynor Law Office, P.C.
Charlottesville, VA

1

Understanding the Divorce Process

Divorces are complicated. There are a number of substantive issues, and there are a number of procedural options involved. The procedures in a divorce case vary greatly based upon whether there is agreement on issues, or whether there are issues in dispute to be resolved by the judge.

A person going through a divorce has to deal with all of the legal complexity at the same time he or she is typically having to deal with strong emotions, disruptions to the home and family life, and the strong emotions of his or her spouse. In short, this is the worst time in your life to have to deal with a very complicated, expensive, demanding legal process.

As you read this book, you will gain a working understanding of the divorce process, procedures, and issues. This chapter will address many of your initial questions regarding the divorce process.

1.1   What steps are taken during the divorce process?

A typical divorce involves a separation, the filing of a complaint for divorce, service of process, responsive pleadings by the other party, discovery, settlement or trial, and the entry of a divorce order. This sounds complicated, but it is made even more complicated by the fact that divorce cases develop in innumerable ways. Some parties settle all issues before they even separate, and then obtain an uncontested, no-fault divorce. At the other end of the spectrum, some parties go to court and have the judge decide all of the issues, such as:

- who is going to remain in the house during the separation
- what the children's schedule will be
- how much support will be paid
- how the property is to be divided

Most common are cases in which the parties are able to agree upon most or all of the issues at some point during the process, before trial.

1.2   Must I have an attorney to get a divorce in Virginia?

Your divorce can either be handled by you and your spouse acting *pro se* (which means without an attorney), or by an attorney. Many divorce cases are handled by attorneys because most divorcing parties are not familiar with the requirements for a divorce, and legal advice cannot be provided by court clerks or other nonlawyers.

1.3   What is my first step?

Most people first fully explore whether the marriage can be saved, especially if there are children. Once divorce appears to be a real possibility, the first step should be to become educated about the process and issues. Reading this book is a good first step. Although reading it can be very helpful, it is not a substitute for the advice provided by a good divorce attorney.

1.4   What is the process for divorce if my spouse and I settle all of our issues by agreement?

One of you will still have to file a complaint for divorce, the lawsuit requirements have to be met—including service or acceptance of process, and presentation of evidence—and a final order of divorce has to be presented to and signed by a circuit court judge.

1.5   Can I divorce my spouse in Virginia if he or she lives in another state?

It depends. Yes, if you last lived in Virginia as husband and wife. In other cases, you should consult with a divorce attorney. (This can be a complicated issue as a Virginia court may have jurisdiction to grant a divorce, but not to make other rulings such as property division.)

1.6 What is required to be *legally separated*?

You cannot be living as husband and wife, and at least one of you has to have the intent to end the marriage to meet the requirements of being *legally separated*. Separation in the same home can meet these requirements, provided you live like roommates rather than like husband and wife. For example, a sexual relationship, socializing together, carrying out other marital duties, and otherwise acting as a married couple would be inconsistent with a legal separation.

1.7 Is a signed document or a court filing required to establish a legal separation?

No.

1.8 If we both want a divorce, does it matter who files?

Either of you can file a complaint for divorce and obtain a divorce (though you may have different grounds of divorce with different waiting periods available to you). If you think your case may go to trial, there may be an advantage to being the first to file.

1.9 Is there a way to keep my divorce private?

As a general rule, lawsuits, including divorce cases, are public records. As a practical matter, unless you are a celebrity, it is unlikely that anyone is going to review your divorce file in the circuit court clerk's office. In rare cases, a motion is made and a judge enters an order to keep a divorce case private.

1.10 What does it mean to *accept service of process*?

Acceptance of service of process is one of the ways to avoid the need to have the sheriff serve the divorce papers. The defendant signs an acceptance of service form before a notary, and, once this form is filed with the court, the service of process requirement is satisfied.

1.11   Why should I contact an attorney if I have received divorce papers?

You need an attorney if your spouse has filed a divorce complaint against you. You need to understand the process, the issues, the possible outcomes, and your options. Once you have been served with a divorce complaint, you have only twenty-one days to respond, so time is of the essence.

1.12   How much notice will I receive if my spouse seeks a temporary order?

A *temporary order,* also known as a *pendente lite order,* governs issues such as custody, visitation, possession of the home, and support until the final divorce order is entered. You should receive at least a week's notice before a hearing on any motion, though in most cases the notice is considerably longer than one week.

1.13   During my divorce, what am I responsible for doing?

That depends upon the attorney you are working with. Some attorneys give extensive homework to clients at the beginning of the process. Other attorneys tailor their requests for information and assistance based upon the client and the case.

Some clients are very capable of and interested in helping, and other clients feel overwhelmed at the beginning of a divorce.

Some clients have access to documentation and information that is needed for the divorce, but sometimes that documentation and information is in the possession of the other party.

Some clients want to do as much as possible to reduce legal costs, and other clients expect their lawyer to handle as much of the work as possible.

Your divorce attorney should meet with you on a regular basis to discuss and agree upon what needs to be done, and how the work is to be allocated between you.

1.14 My spouse has all of our financial information. How will I be able to prepare for negotiations and trial if I don't know the facts or have the documents?

In many cases, the parties and their attorneys cooperate to exchange necessary information. If cooperation is not possible, or to supplement the information exchanged voluntarily, once a divorce complaint is filed you may engage in discovery, which will allow you to obtain necessary information from the other side using certain procedures with time limits.

1.15 My spouse and I both want our divorce to be amicable. How can we keep it that way?

You and your spouse are to be acknowledged for your willingness to cooperate while moving through the divorce process. This will not only make your lives easier and save you money on attorney fees, but it is also more likely to result in an outcome that satisfies you both.

Find a lawyer who understands your goal to reach a settlement and encourage your spouse to do the same. Cooperate in the prompt exchange of necessary information. Ask your attorney about the different negotiation options. Recognize that settlement requires compromise by both parties.

1.16 How long will it take to get my divorce?

A divorce can be obtained approximately eight months after the separation if the parties sign an agreement resolving all issues, there are no minor children, and the attorneys and the parties are prompt in taking the necessary steps. If there are minor children or issues to be resolved by the judge, then the divorce will take over a year to resolve. The actual length of time necessary to obtain a divorce varies, based not just upon the nature of your case, but also on the court schedule in the locality where your divorce case is filed.

1.17 When does my divorce become final?

Your divorce is final once the issues in the case are settled or resolved, and the judge signs the divorce order.

2

Working with Your Attorney

If there is one thing you can be sure of in your divorce, it's that you will be given plenty of advice. Well-intentioned neighbors, cousins, and complete strangers will be happy to tell you war stories about their ex or about their sister who got divorced in New York. Many will give you free advice about what you should do, even though they know little about the facts of your case or the law in Virginia.

There is one person whose advice will matter to you: your attorney. Your lawyer should be your trusted and supportive counselor and advocate throughout your divorce. The advice of your attorney can affect your life for years to come. You will never regret taking the time and making the effort to choose the right attorney for you.

2.1 Where do I begin looking for an attorney for my divorce?

There are many ways to find a divorce lawyer. Ask people you trust—friends and family members who have gone through a divorce—if they thought they had a good lawyer (or if their former spouse did). If you know professionals who work with attorneys, ask for a referral to an attorney who is experienced in family law.

Search the Internet. Most good attorneys have websites that provide information regarding their practices areas, professional associations, experience, and philosophy.

2.2   How do I choose the right attorney?

Choosing the right attorney for your divorce is an important decision. Your attorney should be a trusted professional with whom you feel comfortable sharing information openly. He or she should be a person you can trust, as you will rely upon your attorney to help you make many important decisions throughout the course of your divorce.

Gather at least three names from referrals or the Internet. This short list should include attorneys who practice primarily or solely in the family law area. Next, compare and contrast the attorneys on your short list, seeking the best fit for you and your case.

Determine the level of experience you want in your attorney. For example, if you have had a short marriage, no children, or few assets, an attorney with less experience might be a good value for your legal needs. However, if you are anticipating a custody dispute or have complex or substantial assets, a more experienced attorney may better meet your needs. There is usually a correlation between the years of experience and the hourly rate charged by an attorney.

Look at the websites of each of the attorneys you are considering. Call each of the offices for preliminary information including availability and hourly rates. For each call consider whether you are treated with prompt and professional courtesy.

Consider the qualities in an attorney that are important to you. Even the most experienced and skilled attorney is not right for every person. Ask yourself what you are really looking for in an attorney, so you can make your choice with these standards in mind. Fit is important.

Some attorneys offer a free consultation, especially early in their career when they are in the process of building their practices. The best family law attorneys are busy, so they are unlikely to offer free consultations. Consider interviewing one or more attorneys. You will likely have to pay for these interviews, but it may be worth it for you in terms of finding the best attorney for you and your case.

It is important that you be confident in the attorney you hire. If you are unsure about whether the lawyer is really listening to you or understanding your concerns, keep looking until you find one in whom you have confidence. Your divorce is very likely to be the most important legal matter you will ever have to deal with, so it's critical that you have a professional you can trust.

2.3   Should I hire a "bulldog" — a very aggressive attorney?

Again, consider the qualities in an attorney that are important to you. A "bulldog" may promise to be aggressive and take your spouse for everything he or she is worth, and that approach may suit you. Alternatively, it may be important to you to create a mutually respectful relationship with your spouse during and after the divorce, especially if there are minor children involved.

Additionally, expect the cost of your divorce to exponentially increase if your attorney is unwilling to negotiate and drags your spouse into court at every opportunity. Look for a lawyer who can competently and energetically represent you, while at the same time maintain a high level of courtesy, professionalism, and integrity. The best divorce attorneys know how to effectively represent you in court, but they sincerely seek to assist you in resolving things fairly and by agreement, if possible.

2.4   Should I interview more than one attorney?

Be willing to interview more than one attorney. Every lawyer has different strengths, and it is important that you find the one that is right for you. Sometimes it is only by meeting with more than one attorney that you see clearly who will best be able to help you reach your goals in the way you want. One difficulty is that people going through a divorce change during the process.

Emotion often rules with a stronger hand at the beginning of the process and it is not uncommon for people to dismiss in their minds the possibility of going to court. Then, in some cases, they realize that at least the threat of court is necessary for a fair settlement. That is why in most cases you want an attorney who is a competent trial attorney (and thus a credible threat in the other party's mind), but who wants to also help you settle.

2.5 My spouse says since we're still friends we should use the same attorney for the divorce. Is this possible?

No. An attorney is ethically prohibited from representing both sides in a divorce case.

It is not uncommon for one party to retain an attorney and for the other party not to do so. In such cases, the party with the attorney files the complaint, and agreements reached between the parties are typically sent to the spouse for approval prior to any court hearing. If your spouse has filed for divorce and said that you do not need an attorney, you should nevertheless meet with a lawyer for advice. Sometimes couples reach an agreement without understanding all of their rights under the law. A party will benefit from receiving legal advice on issues such as support, tax considerations, retirement, and health insurance coverage.

2.6 What information should I take with me to the first meeting with my attorney?

Attorneys differ on the amount of information they like to see at an initial consultation. If a court proceeding has already been initiated by either you or your spouse, it is important to take a copy of any court documents.

If you have a prenuptial or postnuptial agreement with your spouse, that is another important document for you to bring to the first meeting.

If you intend to ask for support, either for yourself or for your children, documents evidencing income of both you and your spouse will also be useful. These might include:

- recent pay stubs
- individual and business tax returns, W-2s, and 1099s
- bank statements showing deposits

A statement of your monthly budget will need to be prepared if you or your spouse seek spousal support. Your attorney can provide you with the form that he or she prefers.

If your situation is urgent or you do not have access to these documents, do not let it stop you from scheduling an appointment with an attorney. Prompt legal advice about your rights is often more important than having detailed financial information in the beginning. Your attorney can explain to you the options for obtaining these financial records if they are not readily available to you.

2.7 What unfamiliar words might an attorney use at our meetings?

Law has a language all its own, and divorce law is no exception. Some words you might hear include the following. Additional terms are listed in the glossary.

- *Court*—the judge; the courthouse
- *Divorce*—actual order of divorce, or entire process of divorce
- *Plaintiff*—spouse who files the divorce complaint
- *Defendant*—spouse who did not file the divorce complaint
- *Jurisdiction*—authority of a court to make rulings affecting a party; locality where divorce action is filed
- *Service*—process of formally notifying a party about a legal filing
- *Discovery*—process in which the parties provide information to each other pursuant to court rules
- *Parties*—the divorcing spouses
- *Guardian ad litem*—attorney appointed to represent a child or children

Never hesitate to ask your attorney the meaning of a term. Your complete understanding of your lawyer's advice is essential for you to partner with him or her as effectively as possible.

2.8 What can I expect at an initial consultation with an attorney?

Some attorneys will ask that you complete a questionnaire or an information form prior to or after the first meeting.

The nature of the advice you get from an attorney in an initial consultation will depend upon whether you are still deciding whether you want a divorce, whether you are planning for a possible divorce in the future, whether you are ready to file for divorce right away, or whether a divorce case has already been filed.

During the meeting you will likely discuss the following:
- the history of the marriage
- background information regarding you, your spouse, and your children
- your immediate situation
- your intentions and goals regarding your relationship with your spouse
- any information you are seeking from the attorney
- any questions you may have

You can expect the attorney to provide you with the following information:
- the procedure for divorce in Virginia
- identification of the issues important in your case
- preliminary discussion of the substantive issues
- information regarding him or herself
- information about fees and costs
- initial advice

Although some questions may be impossible for the attorney to answer at the initial meeting because additional information or research is needed, the initial consultation is an opportunity for you to ask all of the questions you have at that time.

2.9 Will the communication with my attorney be confidential?

Yes, your lawyer has an ethical duty to maintain confidentiality regarding you and your case. This duty of confidentiality also extends to the legal staff working with your attorney. Realize, however, that the other party's attorney can gain relevant information from you through discovery requests or by questioning you in court.

2.10 Is there any way that I could waive the attorney-client privilege, as it relates to confidentiality?

Yes. To ensure that communications between you and your attorney remain confidential, and to protect against the voluntary or involuntary waiver of such privilege, below are some tips to consider:

11

- Be careful to talk to only your most trusted friends or family regarding your discussions with your attorney.
- Social media provides the potential for waiving the attorney-client privilege by publicly disclosing confidential information. Do not post information or send messages relating to your case on Facebook, Twitter, or other social media websites.
- Do not post information relating to your case or communications with your attorney on a personal blog, video blog, in online chat rooms, or online message boards.
- Do not use your work-related e-mail to communicate with your attorney, or to discuss your case.
- Depending upon your employer's policy relating to electronic communication, the attorney-client privilege may be waived by communicating with your attorney or by discussing your case through your personal e-mail account (Gmail, Yahoo, etc.) via a company computer. To ensure your communications remain confidential, it is best to only communicate via e-mail from your private e-mail address from a personal and secure computer.
- Do not forward e-mails from your attorney to others, especially not to your spouse.

2.11 Can I take a friend or family member to my initial consultation?

Yes, having someone present during your initial consultation can be a source of great support. You might ask him or her to take notes on your behalf so that you can focus on listening and asking questions. Remember that this is your consultation, and it is important that the attorney hears the facts of your case directly from you. Also, ask your attorney how having a third party present at your consultation could impact the attorney-client privilege. As a minimum, do not make any confessions or disclosures (adultery, for example) with a third party present.

12

2.12   I had an affair and I am uncomfortable admitting this to my attorney. I don't want anyone else to know.

It is important that your attorney know as much as a possible about your case in order to give you the best possible advice.

2.13   Will what I tell my attorney remain confidential?

Your attorney has a duty of confidentiality, so he or she cannot discuss your case with anyone outside of the case. However, your spouse's attorneys can send discovery requests to your attorney seeking information relevant to your case. Absent an exception such as a Fifth Amendment claim, your attorney will have to provide the other attorney with relevant information, even if you would prefer that it not be disclosed. If there is a hearing or trial, the other attorney can question you directly on any issue that is relevant to the case.

2.14   I'm worried that I won't remember to ask my lawyer about all of the issues in my case. How can I be sure I don't miss anything?

Since you are reading this book, you are clearly focused upon being educated regarding the divorce process and issues. Meet with your divorce lawyer on a regular basis. Make a list of developments, facts, and questions to discuss with your attorney. Providing your attorney with written notes will likely save you money and her time as she can read your notes in less time than it would take her to talk to you and make notes.

2.15   What exactly will my attorney do to help me get a divorce?

Your attorney will play a critical role in helping you obtain your divorce. Your attorney may perform any of the following tasks on your behalf:

- Advise you regarding your rights and responsibilities under the law
- Develop a strategy for advising you about all aspects of your divorce
- Assess the case to determine which court has jurisdiction to handle your divorce
- Prepare legal documents for filing with the court

- Counsel you regarding the risks and benefits of negotiated settlement as compared to proceeding to trial
- Inform you of actions you are required to take
- Conduct discovery to obtain information from the other party, which could include depositions, requests for production of documents, and written interrogatories
- Support you in responding to discovery requests from opposing counsel
- Obtain necessary witnesses and documents by serving subpoenas
- Perform financial analysis of your case
- Conduct legal research
- Calendar and keep you advised of all deadlines and court appearances
- Prepare you for court appearances and depositions
- Prepare your case for hearings and trial, including preparing exhibits and interviewing witnesses
- Appear with you at all court appearances, depositions, and conferences
- Assist you with any postdivorce tasks
- Perform other work to assist you in the handling of your divorce case

2.16 What professionals should I expect to work with during my divorce?

Depending upon the issues identified by your attorney, you could possibly work with various professionals, such as appraisers, financial professionals, vocational experts, real estate agents, or mental health experts.

Additionally, in some cases where custody or visitation issues are disputed, the court may appoint a guardian *ad litem*. This lawyer has the duty to represent the best interests of the child. A guardian *ad litem* has the responsibility to investigate you and your spouse as well as the needs of your child, and to advocate on behalf of your child or children.

Another expert who could be appointed by the judge is a psychologist. The role of the psychologist will depend upon the purpose for which he or she is appointed. For example, the psychologist may be appointed to perform a child-custody evaluation, which involves assessing both parents and the child, or this expert may be ordered to provide therapy to members of the family.

In many cases there are no professionals involved except the attorneys for the parties.

2.17   May I bring my children to meetings with my attorney?

It's best to make other arrangements for your children when you meet with your attorney. Your attorney will be giving you a great deal of important information during your conferences, and it will benefit you to give your full attention.

It's also recommended that you keep information about the legal aspects of your divorce from your children. Knowledge that you are seeing an attorney can add to your children's anxiety about the process, and bringing them to your attorney's office involves them too much in the divorce process.

Most law offices are not designed to accommodate young children and are ordinarily not child proof. For both your children's well-being and your own peace of mind, arrange for someone to care for your children when you have meetings with your attorney.

2.18   What is the role of the *paralegal* or *legal assistant* in my attorney's office?

A *paralegal,* or *legal assistant* (the terms are used interchangeably in this book), is a trained legal professional whose duties include providing support for you and your lawyer. Working with a paralegal can make your divorce easier because he or she is likely to be available to communicate with you. It can also lower your legal costs, as the hourly rate for paralegal services is less than the rate for attorneys.

Paralegals are prohibited from giving legal advice. It is important that you respect the limits of the role of the paralegal if he or she is unable to answer your question because it calls for a legal opinion. However, a paralegal can provide the attorney's answers to questions between meetings, and can provide information to you throughout your divorce.

Paralegals can help you by receiving information from you, reviewing documents with you, providing you with updates on your case, working with you on discovery responses, and answering questions about the divorce process that do not call for legal advice.

2.19 My attorney is not returning my phone calls. What can I do?

You have a right to expect your telephone calls to be returned within a reasonable time by your lawyer. Here are some options to consider:

- Ask to speak to the paralegal or another attorney in the office.
- Send an e-mail or fax telling your lawyer that you have been trying to reach him or her by phone and explaining the reason it is important that you receive a call.
- Ask the receptionist to schedule a telephone conference for you to speak with your attorney at a specific date and time.
- Schedule a meeting with your attorney to discuss both the issue needing attention as well as your concerns about the communication.

If your calls are not being returned, take action to get the communication with your lawyer back on track, or consider changing attorneys.

2.20 How do I know when it's time to change lawyers?

The following are questions to ask yourself when you're deciding whether to stay with your attorney or to seek a new lawyer:

- Have I spoken directly to my attorney about my concerns?
- When I expressed concerns, did my lawyer take action accordingly?
- Is my lawyer open and receptive to what I have to say?
- Am I blaming my lawyer for bad behavior of my spouse or opposing counsel?
- Have I provided my lawyer the information needed for taking the next action?

- Does my lawyer have control over the complaints I have, or are they governed by the law or the judge?
- Is my lawyer keeping promises for completing action on my case?
- Do I trust my lawyer?
- What would be the advantages of changing lawyers when compared to the cost?
- Do I believe my lawyer will effectively support me to achieve the outcome I'm seeking in my divorce?

Every effort should be made to resolve your concerns directly with your attorney. If you have made this effort and the situation remains unchanged, it may be time to switch lawyers. Changing lawyers during a divorce is quite common, though you should exercise due diligence and have reasonable expectations to avoid multiple attorney changes once the divorce case has begun.

2.21 Are there certain expectations that I should have when working with my attorney?

Yes. Your attorney will be able to provide you with support and guidance during this process. There are certain actions you can expect of your attorney during your divorce. A list of some of them follows.

Explain the legal process during each step of your case. Understanding the legal process reduces the stress of your divorce. Your attorney can guide you each step of the way.

Listen to your concerns and answer any questions. Although only the attorneys can give you legal advice, everyone on your team (which may consist of a paralegal or a legal assistant and an associate attorney) is available to listen, to provide support, and to direct you to the right person who can help.

Identify important issues, analyze the evidence, and advise you. Divorce is complex. Often there is a great deal of uncertainty. Your attorney can analyze the unique facts of your case and advise you based upon the law and his or her expertise.

Communicate with the opposing party's attorney to try to resolve issues without going to court, and to keep your case progressing. Although your attorney cannot control the actions of the opposing party or his or her lawyer, your attorney can always initiate communication as your advocate. Telephoning, e-mailing, or writing to opposing counsel are actions your attorney can take to encourage cooperation and to keep your divorce moving forward at the pace you want without the expense of contested litigation.

Think creatively regarding challenges with your case and provide options for your consideration. At the outset, you may see many obstacles to reaching a final resolution. Your attorney can offer creative ideas for resolving challenges and help you to explore your options to achieve the best possible outcome.

Facilitate the settlement process. Although your attorney cannot force the other party to settle, your attorney can take action to promote settlement. He or she can prepare settlement proposals, suggest settlement conferences, and negotiate on your behalf.

Support you in developing your custody and visitation arrangements. Many parents do not know how to decide what type of arrangement is best for their children. Your attorney can help you look at the needs of your children and offer advice based on his or her experience in working with families and judges.

Meet with you prior to the filing of a court action and then throughout the proceedings to advise you on actions you should take. There may be important steps to take before you initiate the legal process. Your attorney can help you to be well prepared prior to initiating divorce.

Take action to obtain a temporary court order or to enforce existing orders. Temporary court orders are often needed to ensure clarity regarding rights and responsibilities while your divorce is pending. Your attorney can help you obtain a temporary order and ask the judge to enforce his orders if there is a violation.

Support you in the completion of your discovery responses and preparing for depositions. The discovery process can be overwhelming. You will be asked to provide detailed information and many documents such as income tax returns, property deeds, and child-care costs. Your legal team can make this job easier. If your case involves depositions, your attorney will support you to be fully prepared for the experience.

Help you prepare for hearings and trial, if necessary. Hearings and trial are important and stressful. Proper preparations will reduce your stress, provide you with reasonable expectations, and enable you and your attorney to obtain the best possible outcome.

2.22 Are there certain things my attorney will not be able to do?

Yes, although there are many ways in which your attorney can support you during your divorce, there are also things your attorney will not be able to accomplish.

Force the other parent to exercise his or her parenting time. Your attorney cannot force a parent to exercise parenting time. However, be mindful that a chronic neglect of parenting time may be a basis for modifying your custody and visitation arrangements. Tell your attorney if the other parent is repeatedly failing to exercise his or her parenting time by not showing up, not coordinating visits, or not giving notice of visits.

Force the other party to respond to a settlement proposal. Your attorney may send proposals or make requests to opposing counsel; however, there is no duty to respond. After repeated follow-ups without a response, it may be clear no response is coming. At that time, your attorney will advise you whether the issues merit court action. Both parties must agree on all issues for a case to be settled without a trial. If one party wants to proceed to trial, even over a single issue, he or she will be able to do so.

Control the tone of communication from opposing counsel, or communications from the other party or the other party's family members. Unfortunately, communication from the opposing attorney may sometimes appear rude, condescending, or demanding. Absent a pattern of harassment, your attorney cannot stop the other party or third parties from contacting you. If you do not want the contact, talk with your attorney about how to best handle the situation. Of course, appropriate communication regarding your child or children is always encouraged.

19

Ask the judge to compensate you for every wrong done to you by the other party over the course of your marriage. The judge does not have a free hand to impose the "justice" you may wish to receive. Instead, the judge is limited by the Virginia Code in terms of what she can order in your divorce case. It is important that you learn what the judge can and cannot do, and what outcomes are likely. Work closely with your attorney to develop reasonable expectations.

Remedy poor financial decisions made during the marriage. With few exceptions, the judge's duty is to divide the marital estate as it currently exists. The judge will not attempt to remedy all past financial wrongs, such as overspending or poor investments. If there is significant debt, consult with a debt counselor or bankruptcy lawyer, but make sure to include your divorce attorney in the discussions.

Control how the other party parents your child during his or her parenting time. Each parent has strengths and weaknesses. Absent special circumstances, most judges will not micromanage the parents by issuing orders regarding bedtimes, amount of television watching or video game playing, discipline methods, clothing, or diet.

Demand an accounting of how a parent uses court-ordered child support. The judge will not order a parent to provide an accounting of the use of child support.

Guarantee payment of child support and spousal support. Enforcement of payment of support is only possible when it is court ordered. However, even with a court order, you may experience inconsistent timing of payments due to job loss or a refusal to pay. Talk with your attorney if a pattern of missed payments develops.

Collect child-care and uninsured medical expenses if provisions of the order are not complied with. If your order requires you to provide documentation of payment of expenses to the other party and you fail to do so, you may not be able to collect reimbursement for those expenses. Provide documentation to the other parent as required by court order, even if he or she doesn't pay as required. Always keep a record of the expenses and payments made by each parent, and keep a copy of communications with the other parent regarding payment or

20

reimbursement. It is much easier to keep these records on an ongoing basis than to have to locate and produce copies of old checks, day care bills, medical bills, and insurance documents at a later time.

3

Attorney's Fees and Costs

Any time you make a major investment, you want to know what the cost is going to be and what you are getting for your money. Investing in quality legal representation for your divorce is no different.

The cost of your divorce might be one of your greatest concerns. Because of this, you will want to be an intelligent consumer of legal services. You want quality, but you also want to get the best value for the fees you are paying.

Legal fees for a divorce can be costly and the total expense not predictable. There are actions you can take to control the costs. Develop a plan early on for how you will finance your divorce. Speak openly with your lawyer from the outset about fees. Learn as much as you can about how you will be charged. Insist on a written fee agreement and monthly statements.

By being informed and attentive, your financial investment in your divorce will be money well spent to protect your future.

3.1   Can I get free legal advice from a lawyer over the phone?

Every law firm has its own policy regarding lawyers talking to potential clients. Most questions about your divorce are too complex for a lawyer to give a meaningful answer during a brief telephone conversation.

Questions about your divorce require a review of the facts, circumstances, and background of your marriage. To obtain good legal advice, it's best to schedule an initial meeting with a lawyer who handles divorces.

Some lawyers, as a public service or as a marketing technique, provide a free initial conference, usually limited to thirty minutes. The value of free consultations varies based upon the experience and ability of the attorney.

3.2   Will I be charged for an initial meeting with a lawyer?

It depends. Some lawyers give free consultations, while others charge a fee, usually based upon the attorney's hourly rate. When scheduling your appointment, you should be told the amount of the fee or hourly rate. Payment is ordinarily due at the time of the consultation.

3.3   If I decide to hire an attorney, when do I have to pay him or her?

The answer to this question varies among lawyers. Most divorce attorneys require a retainer in advance of taking any action in the case. Many divorce attorneys require a retainer at or soon after the first meeting.

3.4   What exactly is a *retainer* and how much will mine be?

A *retainer* (as the term is used in the divorce context) is a deposit paid to your lawyer in advance for services to be performed and costs to be incurred in your divorce.

If your case is accepted by the law firm, expect the attorney to request a retainer at or following the initial consultation. The amount of the retainer may vary from hundreds to thousands of dollars, depending upon the nature of your case and the policies of the law firm. Contested custody cases, divorces involving businesses, and interstate disputes, for example, are all likely to require higher retainers.

3.5   Will my attorney accept my divorce case on a *contingency-fee* basis?

No, a *contingency fee* is one that only becomes payable if your case is successful. In Virginia, lawyers are prohibited from entering into a contingent-fee contract in a divorce case. Your lawyer may not accept payment based upon the amount of spousal support or child support awarded or the division of the property.

3.6   How much does it cost to get a divorce?

The cost of your divorce will depend upon many factors. Some attorneys handle no-fault divorces for a flat fee, but most charge by the hour. A *flat fee* is a fixed amount for the legal services being provided. Most Virginia attorneys charge by the hour for divorces. The total cost can vary from under a thousand dollars for a simple, uncontested divorce; to thousands of dollars for a case with some complicated or contested issues; to tens of thousands of dollars (or more) for a complicated or fully litigated case.

It is important that your discussion of the cost of your divorce begin at your first meeting with your attorney. It is customary for family law attorneys to request a retainer prior to beginning work on your case. Be sure to confirm that any unused portion of the retainer is refundable if you do not continue with the case or if you terminate your relationship with the attorney.

3.7   What are typical hourly rates for a divorce lawyer?

In Virginia, attorneys who practice divorce law typically charge hourly rates ranging from $200 per hour to over $400 per hour. The rate your attorney charges will depend upon geographical area, as well as factors such as skills, reputation, experience, and exclusive focus on divorce law.

If you have a concern about the amount of an attorney's hourly rate, but you would like to hire the firm with which the attorney is associated, consider asking to work with an associate attorney in the firm who is likely to charge a lower rate. Associates are attorneys who ordinarily have less experience than the senior attorneys.

3.8   If I can't afford to pay the full amount of the retainer, can I make monthly payments to my attorney?

Every law firm has its own policies regarding payment arrangements. Often these arrangements are tailored to the specific client. Most attorneys will require a substantial retainer to be paid at the outset of your case. Some attorneys may accept monthly payments in lieu of the retainer. Most will require monthly payments in addition to the initial retainer, or request additional retainers as your case progresses. Ask your attorney frank questions to have clarity about your responsibility for payment of legal fees.

3.9 I agreed to pay my attorney a substantial retainer to begin my case. Will I still have to make monthly payments?

Ask your attorney what will be expected of you regarding payments on your account while the divorce is in progress. Obtain a clear understanding of whether monthly payments on your account will be expected, whether it is likely that you will be asked to pay additional retainers, and whether the firm charges interest on past-due accounts. You may be required to keep a minimum credit balance in your account to ensure your case is adequately funded for ongoing legal work.

3.10 My lawyer gave me an estimate of the cost of my divorce, and it sounds reasonable. Do I still need a *written fee agreement?*

Yes, insist upon a *written fee agreement* with your attorney (which most divorce attorneys provide as a standard practice). This is essential not only to define the scope of the services for which you have hired your lawyer, but also to ensure that you have clarity about matters such as your attorney's hourly rate, whether you will be billed for certain costs such as copying, and when you can expect to receive statements on your account.

A clear fee agreement reduces the risk of misunderstandings between you and your lawyer. It supports you both in being clear about your promises to one another so that your focus can be on the legal services being provided rather than on disputes about fees and costs.

3.11 How will I know how the fees and charges are accumulating?

Be sure your written fee agreement with your attorney is completely clear about how you will be informed regarding the status of your account. If your attorney agrees to handle your divorce for a flat fee, your fee agreement should clearly set forth what is included in the fee.

Most attorneys charge by the hour for handling divorces. At the outset of your case, be sure your written fee agreement includes a provision for the attorney to provide you with regular statements of your account. It is reasonable to ask that these be provided monthly.

Review the statement of your account promptly upon receipt. Check to make sure there are no errors, such as duplicate billing entries. If your statement reflects work that you were unaware was performed, call for clarification. Your attorney's office should be helpful in responding to any questions you have about services it provides.

Your statement might also include filing fees, court reporter fees for transcripts of court testimony or depositions, copy expenses, or interest charged on your account. If time has passed and you have not received a statement on your account, call your attorney's office to request one. Legal fees can mount quickly, and it is important that you are aware of the status of your legal expenses.

3.12 What other expenses are related to the divorce litigation besides lawyer fees?

Talk to your attorney about costs other than the attorney fees. Ask whether it is likely there will be filing fees; court reporter expenses, fees for subpoenas; or expert-witnesses, mediation, or parenting class fees. Expert-witness fees can be a substantial expense, ranging from hundreds to thousands of dollars, depending upon the type of expert and the extent to which he or she is involved in your case.

Speak frankly with your attorney about these costs so that together you can make the best decisions about how to allocate your budget for your divorce.

3.13 Who pays for the experts such as appraisers, accountants, psychologists, and mediators?

Costs for the services of experts, whether appointed by the court or hired by the parties, are ordinarily paid for by the parties.

In the case of the guardian *ad litem* who may be appointed to represent the best interests of your children, the amount of the fee will depend upon how much time this professional spends. The judge often orders this fee to be shared by the parties, though depending upon the circumstances, one party can be ordered to pay the entire fee. If you can demonstrate *indigency,* that is, a very low income and no ability to pay, the state may pay your share of the guardian *ad litem* fee.

Psychologists either charge by the hour or set a flat fee for certain types of evaluation. Again, the court can order one party to pay this fee, or both parties to share the expense. It is not uncommon for a psychologist to request payment in advance.

Mediators either charge a flat fee per session or an hourly rate. Generally each party will pay one half of the mediator's fee, though the parties may agree for the entire cost to be paid by the party with the higher income.

The fees for many experts, including appraisers and accountants, will vary depending upon whether they are called upon to provide only a specific service such as an appraisal, or whether they will need to prepare for giving testimony and appear as a witness at trial. Generally each party is responsible for the cost of his or her experts, though the court has the authority to order reimbursement (usually only partial, if at all) from the other party.

3.14 What factors will impact how much my divorce will cost?

Although it is difficult to predict how much your legal fees will be, the following are some of the factors that affect the cost:

- whether there are children
- whether child custody is agreed upon
- whether there are complicated legal or factual questions
- whether a pension plan will be divided between the parties
- the nature of the issues contested
- the financial complexity of the case

- the number of issues agreed to by the parties
- the level of cooperation between the parties and counsel
- the frequency and effectiveness of your communications with your attorney
- the willingness and ability of the parties to communicate constructively with each other
- the promptness with which information is provided and exchanged between both the clients and the attorneys
- whether there are litigation costs, such as fees for expert witnesses or court reporters
- the hourly rate of the attorney
- the time it will take to conclude your divorce
- the number of court appearances required to resolve all disputes between the parties

3.15   Will my attorney charge for phone calls and e-mails?

Unless your case is being handled on a flat-fee basis (which is very rare for any divorce other than a simple, uncontested divorce), you should expect to be billed for any communication with your attorney. Many of the professional services provided by lawyers are handled by telephone and by e-mail. This time can be spent giving legal advice, negotiating, and gathering or sharing information to protect and further your interests. These calls and e-mails are all legal services for which you should anticipate being charged by your attorney.

To make the most of your time during attorney telephone calls, plan your call in advance. Organize the information you want to relay, your questions, and any concerns to be addressed. This will help you to be clear and focused during the telephone conversation to avoid wasting time.

3.16   Will I be charged for talking to the staff at my lawyer's office?

It depends. Check the terms of your fee agreement with your lawyer. Whether you are charged for talking to nonlawyer members of the law office may depend upon their role in the office. If you are charged it should be at a rate significantly lower than an attorney's rate.

Your lawyer's support staff will be able to relay your messages and receive information from you. They may also be able to answer many of your questions. The effective use of paralegals, legal assistants, and associate attorneys is an important way to control your legal costs.

3.17 What is a *trial retainer* and will I have to pay one?

The purpose of the *trial retainer* is to fund the work needed to prepare for trial and for services the day or days of trial. A trial retainer is a sum of money paid in advance on your account with your lawyer when it appears as though your case may not settle and may proceed to trial.

Confirm with your attorney that any unearned portion of your trial retainer will be refunded if your case settles. Ask your lawyer whether and when a trial retainer might be required in your case so that you can plan your budget accordingly.

3.18 How do I know whether I should settle versus go to trial?

Deciding whether to take a case to trial or to settle is often a challenging point in the divorce process. This decision should be made with the support of your attorney. Though there may be some lawyers who would prefer trial to settlement, the great majority of divorce lawyers are sincerely interested in helping you reach a fair settlement.

When the issues in dispute are primarily financial, often the decision about settlement is related to the costs of going to trial. Be clear about just how far apart you and your spouse are on the financial matters and compare this to the estimated costs of going to trial. By comparing these amounts, you can decide whether a compromise on certain financial issues, and certainty about the outcome, would be better than paying legal fees and taking the risk of going to trial.

3.19 Is there any way I can reduce some of the expenses of getting a divorce?

Litigation of any kind can be expensive, and divorces are no exception. However, there are many ways that you can help control the expense, including the following:

Put it in writing. If you need to relay information that is important but not urgent, consider providing it to your attorney by mail, fax, or e-mail. This creates a prompt and accurate record for your file and takes less lawyer time than providing the information orally. Attorneys can read faster than they can listen to you and make notes.

Keep your attorney informed. Just as your attorney should keep you up to date on the status of your case, you need to do the same. Keep your lawyer advised about any major developments in your life such as plans to move, to have someone move into your home, to change your employment status, to buy or sell property, or to begin dating.

If your contact information changes during your divorce, be sure to notify your attorney.

Obtain a copy of documents. An important part of litigation includes reviewing documents such as tax returns, account statements, report cards, and medical records. Your attorney will ordinarily be able to request or subpoena these items, but many may be readily available to you directly or upon request to your spouse. The more tasks you handle yourself, the more you save.

Consult your attorney's website. If your lawyer has a website, it may be a great source of useful information. The answers to commonly asked questions about the divorce process can often be found there, saving you the cost of speaking with the attorney.

Utilize support professionals. Get to know the support staff at your lawyer's office. Although only attorneys are able to give you legal advice, the receptionist, paralegal, or legal assistant may be able to answer your questions regarding the status of your case. All of your communications with any employee of the law firm are required to be kept confidential.

Consider working with an associate attorney. Although the senior attorneys in a law firm may have more experience, you may find that working with an associate attorney is a good option. Hourly rates for an associate attorney are typically lower than those charged by a senior attorney. Frequently the associate attorney has trained under a senior attorney and developed the necessary skills and knowledge of the law.

Discuss with the firm the relative benefits of working with a senior versus an associate attorney in light of the nature of your case, the experience and expertise of the respective attorneys, and the potential cost savings to you.

Leave a detailed message. If your attorney knows the information you are seeking, he or she can often get the answer before returning your call. This not only gets your answer faster, but also reduces costs.

Discuss more than one matter during a call. It is not unusual for clients to have many questions during litigation. If your question is not urgent, consider waiting to call until you have more than one issue to discuss. Never hesitate to call to ask any pressing questions.

Provide timely responses to information requests. Whenever possible, provide information requested by your lawyer in a timely manner. This avoids the cost of follow-up action by your lawyer and the additional expense of extending the time in litigation.

Remain open to settlement. The best way to reduce your costs in a divorce case is to settle issues and reduce conflict. Recognize that when your disagreement concerns financial matters, the value of money in dispute may be less than the amount it will cost to go to trial. Be reasonable in seeking and agreeing to fair compromises.

3.20 I don't have any money, and I need a divorce. What are my options?

The options for free legal services are very limited. If you have a low income and few assets, you may be eligible to obtain a divorce at no cost or minimal cost through one of the Legal Aid offices in the state. Legal Aid has a screening process for potential clients, as well as limits on the nature of the cases it takes. The demand for its services is usually greater than the number of attorneys available to handle cases.

If you have other issues to resolve as part of your divorce case, such as custody or a protective order, Legal Aid is unlikely to be able to help.

3.21 I don't have much money, but I need to get a divorce. What should I do?

Consider some of these options:

- Borrow the legal fees from friends or family. Often those close to you are concerned about your future and may be willing to support you in your goal of having your rights protected. If the retainer is too much money to request from a single individual, consider whether a handful of persons might each be able to contribute a lesser amount to help you reach your goal of hiring a lawyer.

- Charge the legal fees on a low-interest credit card or consider taking out a loan.

- Start saving. If your case is not urgent, consider developing a plan for saving the money you need to proceed with a divorce. Your attorney may be willing to receive and hold monthly payments until you have paid an amount sufficient to meet the initial retainer requirement.

- Talk to your attorney about using money held in a joint account with your spouse.

- Find an attorney who will work with you on a monthly payment basis.

- Ask your attorney about your spouse paying for your legal fees. This is usually not a good option as your spouse would rarely have to pay all of your fees, and a court hearing or trial would be necessary to get a court ruling on the issue of attorney's fees if your spouse does not agree.

- Ask your attorney about being paid from the proceeds of the property settlement. If you and your spouse have acquired substantial assets during the marriage, you may be able to find an attorney who will wait to be paid until the assets are divided at the conclusion of the divorce.

Even if you do not have the financial resources to proceed with your divorce at this time, consult with an attorney to learn your rights and to develop an action plan for steps you can take between now and the time you are able to proceed. Often there are measures you can take right away to protect yourself until you have the money to proceed with your divorce.

3.22 Is there anything I can do on my own to get support for my children if I don't have money for a lawyer?

Yes, if you need support for your children, contact the *Virginia Division of Child Support Enforcement (DCSE)* for help in obtaining a child-support order. Although they cannot help you with matters such as custody or property division, they can pursue support from the other parent for your children, at no charge to you.

Call the Virginia Division of Child Support Enforcement Call Center at (800) 468-8894 (Monday through Friday, 7 A.M.–6 P.M., toll-free) or visit their website at: www.dss.virginia.gov/family/dcse/index.cgi.

3.23 If my mother pays my legal fees, will my lawyer give her private information about my divorce?

If someone else is paying your legal feels, discuss with your lawyer, and the person paying, your expectations that your lawyer will honor the ethical duty of confidentiality. Without your permission, your attorney should not disclose information to others about your case. In most cases, the person paying the attorney will want to review the attorney's monthly statements which will contain an itemized and detailed description of the work provided by the law firm on your behalf.

If you authorize your attorney to speak with your family members, be aware that you will be charged for those communications. Regardless of the opinions of the person who pays your attorney fees, your lawyer's ethical duty is to remain your advocate.

3.24 Can I ask the judge to order my spouse to pay my attorney fees?

Yes. If you want to ask the judge to order your spouse to pay any portion of your legal fees, be sure to discuss this with your attorney and he or she will explain your chances of success. Realize that you remain liable for your attorney's fees, even if there is a chance that you will receive a partial reimbursement from your spouse.

If your case is likely to require costly experts and your spouse has a much greater ability to pay these expenses than you, talk to your lawyer about the possibility of filing a motion with the court asking your spouse to pay all or part of these costs while the case is pending.

3.25 What happens if I don't pay my attorney the fees I promised to pay?

Your attorney may seek to withdraw from representation if you do not comply with the fee agreement. Your attorney may also file an attorney's lien against any judgment awarded to you to pay any outstanding attorney's fees or costs to the firm. Consequently, it is important that you keep the promises you have made regarding your account.

If you are having difficulty paying your attorney's fees, talk with your attorney about payment options. Consider borrowing the funds, using your credit card, or asking for help from friends and family.

Above all, do not avoid communication with your attorney if you are unable to stay current with your payments. Staying in touch with your attorney is essential for you to have an advocate throughout your divorce.

4

Initial Issues
Associated with Separation

It is not unusual for a person to realize that he or she is going to get divorced, but has no idea how it's going to work. Who moves out and who stays? What if there is no agreement on how to handle the divorce? What if there is not even an agreement to get divorced? This chapter answers many of those common initial questions.

4.1   My spouse left home weeks ago. I don't want a divorce because I feel our marriage can be saved. Should I still see an attorney?

It's a good idea to see an attorney. Whether you want a divorce or not, your spouse may initiate divorce, so there may be important actions for you to take now to protect your assets, credit, home, children, and future right to support.

4.2   My husband and I are going to divorce, but he won't move out. What do I do?

This is often an issue for divorcing couples. Absent violence, neither party is required to move out based upon the other's request. The best option may be to separate in the same house while obtaining legal advice about your situation and your options. Though the judge has the authority to award the house to one party or the other once a divorce case is filed, in most cases the issue of who moves out is handled by the parties without a court ruling.

4.3   I am thinking about moving out. Should I talk to a lawyer first?

Yes, you should definitely talk to a lawyer before you move from the marital home. There may be consequences of which you are unaware. It is especially important that you obtain legal advice if you want to obtain the house as part of the divorce, if spousal support is an issue, or if custody and visitation are in dispute.

4.4   If either my spouse or I file for divorce, will I be ordered out of my home? Who decides who gets to live in the house while we go through the divorce?

If you and your spouse cannot reach an agreement regarding which of you will leave the residence during the divorce, the judge will decide whether one of you should be granted exclusive possession of the home until the case is concluded. Some judges have been known to refuse to order either party out of the house until the divorce is concluded.

Abusive behavior is one basis for seeking temporary possession of the home. If there are minor children, the custodial parent will ordinarily be awarded temporary possession of the residence.

Other factors the judge may consider include:

- Whether one of you owned the home prior to the marriage
- After provisions are made for payment of temporary support, who can afford to remain in the home or obtain other housing
- Who is most likely to be awarded the home in the divorce
- Options available to each of you for other temporary housing, including other homes or family members who live in the area
- Special needs that would make a move unduly burdensome, such as a health condition
- Self-employment from home, which could not be readily moved, such as a child-care business

If staying in the home is important to you, talk to your attorney about your reasons so that a strong case can be made for you at the temporary hearing.

4.5   My wife gave me a document that indicates that we are separating by mutual consent. Should I sign it?

You should obtain legal advice from a divorce lawyer before you sign any document associated with your divorce to make sure you understand the consequences. For example, you may not want to sign a document that indicates you are separating by mutual consent if your wife is asking for the divorce, and if she is seeking spousal support against you.

4.6   My husband and I are going to divorce. I can't afford to move out, but he scares me with his aggressive behavior. What should I do?

This can be a difficult situation. If your spouse is violent with you, or if he tries to limit, block, or control your movements, you should consider calling 911. (Only do so if absolutely necessary if your children are present, as it is traumatic for children to witness a parent being arrested.) In other situations, obtain legal advice to identify your options, and to discuss the pros and cons of each option.

4.7   I am planning to move out with the children. My parents, who live in Baltimore, have invited me to move in with them. Can I move the children to Maryland?

Absent a court order governing custody and visitation, either party has the legal right to move with the children, but it is rarely a good idea to move (other than locally) with the children without agreement of the other parent or permission of the judge. The other spouse has the option of filing a request with the court that you be ordered to return the children immediately, and these requests are often granted. If you want to move the children some distance from the other parent, it is better to communicate your plans to the other parent in advance. If you cannot agree, then the issue can be determined by a judge.

4.8   Things have gotten so bad at home that I want to go stay with a friend for a few days. Would that be considered desertion?

No, staying with a friend for a few days does not constitute desertion of your spouse or family. It is better to avoid staying with a friend of the opposite sex, especially if you have a romantic or sexual interest in the friend. (This sounds obvious, but you would be surprised.)

4.9   All of my money is in a joint account with my spouse, and I'm worried she is going to empty the account. Should I take the money first?

That is a tough decision. It is best if both parties behave in a predictable, mature, and thoughtful manner. But you would be frustrated if you took the high road and she emptied the account. One option to consider is having a freeze placed on the account so that funds can be withdrawn only if you both agree in writing. Another option is to move one half of the funds into an account in your name.

4.10   My marriage is over, and I'm interested in a coworker who is recently separated. There's no harm in us having lunch together, is there?

You should talk to a divorce lawyer before you start dating. As a general rule, you should postpone dating until your divorce is resolved. You should recognize that it is better to settle your divorce issues, and a settlement is often made more difficult by the emotions associated with the involvement of a new boyfriend or girlfriend. If you have children, realize that the relationship between them and a future significant other is made more difficult if your significant other enters the scene during rather than after the divorce.

4.11   My spouse is a spender, and I'm a saver. We are in the process of separating. What should I do to protect myself?

You should consider a freeze of your joint accounts, or a transfer of one half of the funds to avoid your spouse improperly spending marital assets. You should also consider closing joint credit cards or other lines of credit. Some credit card companies will only close a joint credit card upon the request of both parties. In that case, send a letter to the company and advise it that you do not agree to be liable for any future charges. Keep a file copy of your letter.

4.12 My wife moved in with her parents and I am stuck paying all of the bills. Doesn't she have to pay her share?

Try to agree upon a fair division of the marital bills and other financial arrangements pending the divorce. If you cannot agree, the judge has the authority to allocate the bills between you. That would require the filing of a divorce action, and the scheduling of a court hearing.

4.13 My wife moved out with the children and won't let me see my children. What can I do?

Hire an attorney and have your attorney contact your spouse or her attorney. Your spouse needs to realize that it is not in the children's best interests to not be allowed to see you. In addition, her interference with your relationship with the children can be held against her by the judge. If there is a guardian *ad litem*, seek his or her involvement in the process. If no guardian *ad litem* has been appointed, consider having your attorney request one. Finally, if the other options don't work, schedule a custody and visitation hearing.

4.14 Should I hire a private detective to prove my spouse is having an affair?

That depends upon the specific facts of your case. Adultery can be important if spousal support is an issue. It may also make sense for you to incur this expense if there is a significant amount of money at stake in the divorce. If spousal support is not an issue, and if you and your spouse have a modest net worth, it may not be worth the cost. Discuss this question with your attorney.

4.15 My spouse and I share a home computer on which I send and receive e-mail. Should I have any concerns about this?

Yes, it is very important that any communications you have with your attorney involving your divorce are secure and beyond your spouse's access. There are many tools available (most of which are illegal) for your spouse to access your communications on a shared computer. As a general rule, you should avoid any confidential communications on any device that your spouse can physically access. In addition, you should change all of your passwords and use a combination of letters, numbers, and symbols.

4.16 I have an active Facebook page. Should I have any concerns about this?

Yes, you should limit or suspend your Facebook activities during the divorce. Information posted on Facebook, by you or others, could be used by the other party to gain information to use against you during the divorce.

4.17 If our case ends up going to court, what will the judge learn about my communications with my spouse?

Everything you say or write can be repeated or shown to the judge if you end up in court. It is common for parties to say or write things, especially early in the process before they hire attorneys, that are later used against them. Strive to always be polite and cooperative in your communications with your spouse, for two reasons. First, if you both use that approach, your divorce will be more civil, less stressful, and less expensive. Second, such an approach will help your image with the judge if your case ends up going to court.

4.18 I am concerned that my spouse seems to know what I am doing and where I am going. What can I do?

Technology now allows a person to be tracked in multiple ways (many of which are illegal). Be aware that there are small GPS devices that can be placed on your automobile and used by the other party to track your car's movements. Talk to your attorney about your concerns. You may want to have your car examined by your mechanic for such devices.

Smartphones can be accessed remotely to track movements of the phone, to access e-mails and texts, and even to listen to conversations. You should have your own cell phone plan, and consider a new phone.

4.19 Who is responsible for paying credit card bills and making house payments during the divorce proceedings?

This issue is usually resolved by agreement between spouses based upon who is liable on the account, who has been paying the bill, who is in the house, and other factors. If you can't agree, then this issue can be determined by the judge at a *pendente lite* hearing (a hearing early in the process to resolve temporary issues pending the resolution of the divorce case). Realize that the creditor is not bound by agreements between you and your spouse (for example, if you are liable on a credit card and your spouse agrees to pay but doesn't pay, the company can still pursue you to collect).

4.20 What, if anything, should I be doing with the credit card companies as we go through the divorce?

You should consider closing credit card accounts for which you are responsible and to which your spouse has access. If the company will not close the account without your spouse's consent, send the company a letter (and keep a copy) advising it that you do not agree to be responsible for any future charges.

5

Coping with Stress
during the Divorce Process

It may have been a few years ago, or it may have been many years ago. When you said, "I do," you meant it. Like most people getting married, you planned to be a happily married couple for life.

But things happen. Life brings change. People change. Whatever the circumstances, you now find yourself considering divorce. The emotions of divorce run from one extreme to another as you journey through the process. You may feel relief and an eagerness to move on with your life. On the other hand, you may feel emotions that are quite painful: anger, fear, sorrow, depression, embarrassment, and anxiety. Many people going through divorce feel a deep sense of loss or failure. It is important to find support for coping with all these strong emotions. Especially if you have children, you have to find a way to carry on with your life and obligations.

Because going through a divorce is almost always an exceptionally emotional time, having a clear understanding of the divorce process and what to expect will help you make better decisions.

5.1   The thought of going to a lawyer's office to talk about divorce is more than I can bear. I canceled the first appointment I made because I just couldn't do it. What should I do?

Many people going through a divorce are dealing with lawyers for the first time and feel anxious about the experience. Ask a trusted friend or family member to go with you. He or she can support you by writing down your questions in advance, by taking notes for you during the meeting, and by helping you to remember what the lawyer said after the meeting is concluded. It is likely that you will feel relieved just to be better informed and protected.

5.2   There is some information about my marriage that I think my attorney needs, but I'm too embarrassed to discuss it. Must I tell the attorney?

Your attorney has an ethical duty to maintain confidentiality. Attorneys who practice divorce law are accustomed to hearing intimate information about families. Although it is deeply personal to you, it is unlikely that anything you tell your lawyer will be a shock to him or her. It may feel uncomfortable initially, but it is important that your attorney have complete information so that your interests can be fully protected.

5.3   I'm unsure about how to tell our children about the divorce, and I'm worried I'll say the wrong thing. What's the best way?

How you talk to your children about the divorce will depend upon their ages and development. Changes in your children's everyday lives, such as a change of residence or one parent leaving the home, are very important to them and will have to be discussed. Children, especially younger children, should be shielded from information about legal proceedings and meetings with lawyers.

Simpler answers are best for young children. Avoid giving them more information than they need. Use the adults in your life—not your children—as a source of support to meet your own emotional needs.

Avoid being negative with your children towards their other parent. Recognize that though your marriage is ending, your children need, for their emotional health, to continue to have the best possible relationship with both of their parents. Don't try to undercut your children's relationship with the other parent, no matter how bad your own relationship is with your spouse.

After the initial discussion, keep the door open to further talks by creating opportunities for your children to talk about the divorce. Use these times to acknowledge their feelings and offer support. Always assure them that the divorce is not their fault and that they are still loved by both you and your spouse, regardless of the divorce.

5.4   My youngest child seems very depressed about the divorce, the middle one is angry, and my teenager is skipping school. How can I cope?

A child's reaction to divorce will vary depending upon his or her age and other factors. Some may cry and beg for a reconciliation, and others may behave inappropriately. Reducing conflict with your spouse, being a consistent and nurturing parent, and making sure both of you remain involved are all actions that can support your children regardless of how they are reacting to the divorce.

Support groups for children whose parents are divorcing are also available through some schools and religious communities. A school counselor may be able to provide some support. If more help is needed, consider hiring a therapist experienced in working with children.

Research shows that an important factor in predicting a child's response to a divorce is the level of conflict between the parents. For your children's sake, you should do everything you can to minimize your conflict with the other parent.

5.5   I am so frustrated by my spouse's "Disneyland parent" behavior. Is there anything I can do to stop this?

Feelings of guilt, competition, or remorse sometimes lead a parent to fill parenting time with trips to the toy store and special activities. These feelings can also result in too little discipline expected of the child.

Shift your focus from the other parent's behavior to your own, and do your best to be an outstanding parent during your time with the child. This includes keeping a routine for your child for family meals, bedtime, chores, and homework. Encourage family activities as well as individual time with each child.

During the time when a child's life is changing, providing a consistent and stable routine in your home can ease his or her anxiety and provide comfort.

5.6   Between requests for information from my spouse's lawyer and my own lawyer, I am totally overwhelmed. How do I manage gathering all of this detailed information by the deadlines imposed?

First, simply get started. Often the thought of a task is worse than the job itself.

Second, break it down into smaller tasks. Perhaps one evening you gather your tax returns and on the weekend you work on your monthly living expenses.

Third, seek support. Family members and friends are often willing to help in times of need.

Finally, communicate with your lawyer. Your attorney may be able to make your job easier by giving you suggestions or help. It may be that essential information can be provided now and the details submitted later.

5.7   I am so depressed about my divorce that I'm having difficulty getting out of bed in the morning to care for my children. What should I do?

Take good care of yourself: eat a good diet, exercise daily—even a walk helps—and get enough sleep. Reach out to friends and family; a support network is important during this stressful time in your life. Although feelings of sadness are common during a divorce, more serious depression means it's time to seek professional support. Start with visiting your physician to address any physical health concerns.

Your health and your ability to care for your children are both essential. Follow through on recommendations by your doctor and mental health professional for therapy, medication, exercise, or other measures to improve your wellness and functioning.

5.8   Will taking prescription medication for my anxiety and depression hurt my case?

You should do your best to take care of yourself and your children, and your case is best served by that approach. The use of medicine to treat anxiety and depression is so common that it is unlikely that a judge would hold that against you. Follow your doctor's and your therapist's recommendations and prescriptions carefully.

5.9   I talk a lot about my divorce with several friends and my sister, but it seems that it makes me even more stressed and angry.

You need the support of family and friends while going through a divorce. Unfortunately, well-meaning family members and friends often make things worse with their frustration, anger, and bad advice. Rely on your divorce attorney for advice. Your best approach with your supporters may be to focus on shared interests and other positive things. A constant focus on the negatives of your divorce and the other party is not helpful. Seek positive supporters, and be mindful that you and your children benefit if you stay focused on working through issues and moving forward in a positive and constructive manner.

5.10   I'm the one who filed for divorce, but I still have loving feelings toward my spouse and feel sad about divorcing. Does this mean I should dismiss my divorce?

Strong feelings of caring about your spouse often persist after a divorce is filed. Whether or not to proceed with a divorce is a deeply personal decision, so only you can decide this. Here are several questions to consider:

- Have you and your spouse participated in marriage counseling?
- Has your spouse refused to seek treatment for an addiction?
- Are you worried about the safety of you or your children if you remain in the marriage?
- Is your spouse involved in another relationship?
- Is your spouse committed to the marriage?
- Is there any reasonable prospect that the marital problems that led you to file for divorce can be overcome?

One option to consider is putting the divorce process on hold for so long as you are in doubt.

5.11   Will my lawyer charge me for the time I spend talking about my feelings about my spouse and my divorce?

Yes. It would be difficult to go through a divorce without any discussion with your lawyer about your feelings associated with the divorce. Lawyers vary in their capacity to provide counseling. Some divorce lawyers are helpful, while others prefer to stay more narrowly focused on the legal issues. But realize that counselors and therapists typically charge at a lower hourly rate than your lawyer.

5.12 My lawyer doesn't seem to realize how difficult my divorce is for me. How can I get him to understand?

Some lawyers are more empathetic than others. You want a competent divorce lawyer who is also a good fit regarding your need for empathy. If you feel that your lawyer is not empathetic enough, you can discuss the issue with him, change lawyers, or focus on having your emotional needs met by a counselor and your family and friends.

5.13 I've been told not to speak badly about my spouse in front of my child, but I know my spouse is doing this all the time. Why can't I just speak the truth?

It's harmful to your child to hear either parent being negative about the other parent. Regardless of what the other parent is doing, you should always do what is best for your child (and not just what would give you a momentary satisfaction of retaliation against the other parent). One of the worst things you can do to your child is to bring them into a war with the other parent. First, don't fight with the other parent. Second, if you can't find a way to reduce the conflict despite your best efforts, at least try to shield your child from the hostility, anger, conflict, and unpleasant words. Children should feel free and encouraged to love both of their parents without the need to choose sides.

5.14 I am terrified of having my deposition taken. My spouse's lawyer is very aggressive, and I'm afraid I'm going to say something that will hurt my case. What should I do?

Your deposition is an opportunity for your spouse's attorney to gather information and to assess the type of witness you would be if the case proceeds to trial. Feeling anxious about your deposition is normal.

Remember that your attorney will be seated by your side at all times to support you. You should meet with your lawyer in advance to prepare for the deposition. If you are worried about certain questions that might be asked, talk to your attorney about them in advance. Think of it as an opportunity to move your case closer to completion, and enlist your lawyer's support in being well prepared.

5.15 I am still so angry at my spouse. How can I be expected to sit in the same room during a settlement conference?

If you are still really angry at your spouse, it may be beneficial to postpone the conference for a time. You might also consider counseling to help you cope with your feelings of anger.

Another option might be "shuttle" negotiations. With this method, you and your attorney remain in one room while your spouse and his or her attorney are in another. Settlement offers are then relayed between the attorneys throughout the negotiation process. By shifting your focus from your angry feelings to your goal of a settlement, it may be easier to handle the process.

5.16 I'm afraid I can't make it through court without having an emotional breakdown. How do I prepare?

A divorce trial can be a highly emotional time, though typically it follows a lengthy period of separation. Some of these ideas may help you through the process:

- Meet with your lawyer, usually multiple times, in advance of your court date to prepare for trial.

- Ask your lawyer whether there are any documents you should review in preparation for court, such as your deposition or trial exhibits.

- Get directions, visit the courtroom in advance, and maybe even observe another proceeding.

- Consider having a support person with you in court for your trial.

- Avoid alcohol, eat a good diet, exercise, and have plenty of rest during the period of time leading up to the court date. Each of these will help you to prepare for the emotions of the day.

- Plan what you intend to wear in advance. Small advance preparations may lower your stress.
- Visualize the experience going well. Picture yourself sitting in the witness chair, giving clear, confident, and truthful answers to questions.
- Arrive early at the courthouse, and make sure you have a plan for parking your car if you are not familiar with the area.
- Take slow, deep breaths. Breathing deeply will steady your voice, calm your nerves, and improve your focus.
- Realize that your attorney will be your advocate and support throughout the proceedings.

6

Emergency: When You
Fear Your Spouse

Suddenly you are in a panic. Maybe your spouse was serious when threatening to take your child and leave the state. What if you're kicked out of your own home? Suppose all of the bank accounts are emptied? Your anxiety increases as you think about the bad stories you've heard about divorce.

Facing an emergency situation in divorce, you may be paralyzed with fear and have no idea how to begin to protect yourself. No doubt you have countless worries about what your future holds.

Remember that you have overcome many challenges in your life before this moment. There are people willing to help you. Step-by-step, you will make it through this time as well.

When facing an emergency, do your best to focus on what to do in the immediate moment. Stay calm, obtain advice from your divorce lawyer, and make good decisions.

6.1 My spouse has deserted me, and I don't have enough money to pay my bills and buy food. What is my first step?

Your first step is to call upon family and friends for temporary financial help until a support order can be entered. Next, seek legal advice at your earliest opportunity. The sooner you get legal counsel to advise you about your options, the better. Support can be ordered in Virginia by either your local juvenile and domestic relations district court or by your local circuit court. Your lawyer will identify and discuss options with you, and help you choose the course of action that is best for you given the facts of your case and the specific options available.

6.2 I'm afraid my abusive spouse will try to hurt me or our children if I say I want a divorce. What can I do to protect myself and my children?

Develop a plan with your safety and that of your children as your highest priority. In addition to meeting with an attorney, develop a safety plan in the event you and your children need to escape your home.

Your risk of harm from an abusive spouse may increase when you leave with the children. For this reason, all actions must be taken with safety as the first concern.

Find a lawyer who understands domestic violence. Talk to your lawyer about the concerns for your safety and that of your children.

If domestic violence occurs, call 911 immediately. Based upon the situation, this may result in criminal charges being placed and a protective order being entered.

6.3 Will a protective order keep me safe?

Unfortunately, there is no guarantee that a protective order will keep you safe. A protective order will help only if your spouse is concerned with abiding by the law. But in some cases a spouse is intent on doing harm without regard for the consequences. In that situation, a protective order will not help. Murder and suicide, though rare, do occur in connection with divorces. If you are in such a dangerous relationship, it is imperative that you think through carefully every step of the process to minimize the chance of a tragedy.

6.4 I want to give my attorney all the information needed so my children and I are safe from my spouse. What does this include?

Provide your attorney with complete information about the history, background, nature, and evidence of the abuse you have suffered including:

- the types of abuse (for example, physical, sexual, verbal, financial, mental, emotional)
- the dates, time frames, or occasions

- the locations
- whether you were ever treated medically
- whether a 911 call was placed and any police reports made
- e-mails, letters, notes, or journal entries
- any photographs taken
- any witnesses to the abuse or evidence of the abuse
- any statements made by your spouse admitting the abuse
- alcohol or drug abuse
- the presence of guns or other weapons

The more complete the information you provide to your lawyer, the easier it will be for him or her to provide you with advice and to make a strong case for the protection of you and your children.

6.5 What documents or items should I give my attorney to help prove the history of domestic violence by my spouse?

The following may be useful exhibits if your case goes to court:

- photographs of injuries
- photographs of damaged property
- abusive or threatening notes, letters, texts, or e-mails
- abusive or threatening voice messages
- police reports
- medical records
- court records
- criminal records
- damaged property, such as torn clothing

Tell your attorney which of these you have or are able to obtain, and ask whether others can be acquired through a subpoena or other means.

6.6   I'm not ready to hire a lawyer for a divorce, but I am afraid my spouse is going to get violent with my children and me in the meantime. What can I do?

Once violence occurs and the police are called, you will be provided advice by the police, the prosecutor, or the victim coordinator regarding prosecution of your spouse and the option for a protective order. Unfortunately, there is little that can be done, from a legal perspective, in advance of violence, unless there are specific and current threats of harm.

6.7   When can I obtain a *restraining* or *protective order*?

A *protective* or *restraining order* is a court order directing a person to not engage in certain behavior. Although the order can initially be obtained without notice to the other person, there is always a right to a hearing to determine whether a protective order or restraining order should remain in place.

You can consider obtaining a protective order if you are reasonably concerned about your safety or your children's safety. If your spouse has attempted to cause or has caused you bodily injury, or has threatened to cause you bodily injury, you may qualify for a protective order. A general concern not based upon specific recent behavior or threats is not sufficient.

The violation of a protective order is a criminal offense which can result in immediate arrest.

6.8   My spouse has been harassing me since I filed for divorce. What can I do?

If your spouse is annoying, threatening, harassing, or intimidating you after your divorce complaint is filed, you should advise your lawyer, and he can discuss your concerns with the other attorney. In addition, protective language can be included in the temporary *(pendente lite)* order that can be entered early in your divorce case.

6.9   I'm afraid my spouse is going to take all of the money out of the bank accounts and leave me with nothing. What can I do?

Talk to your attorney immediately. There are several options to consider. First, you could seek to have the accounts frozen so that no funds can be removed without the written consent of both parties. Second, you could take one half of the funds and put them in an account in your name. Third, you could take all of the funds yourself. This third option is generally not recommended because of the negative consequences that will likely follow (neither the judge nor the other party will appreciate such aggressive behavior). Fourth, you could seek a court order that freezes certain marital accounts not needed for normal living expenses.

6.10   My spouse says that I am crazy, that I am a liar, and that no judge will ever believe me if I tell the truth about the abusive behavior. What can I do if I don't have any proof?

Most domestic violence is not witnessed by third parties. Often there is little physical evidence. Even without physical evidence, a judge can enter orders to protect you and your children if you give truthful testimony about your abuse which the judge finds believable. Your own testimony of abuse is evidence.

It is very common for persons who abuse others to claim that their victims are liars and to make statements intended to discourage disclosure of the abuse. This is yet another form of controlling behavior.

Your attorney's skills and experience will be needed to assist you in providing effective testimony in the courtroom to establish your case. Let your lawyer know your concerns so that a strong case can be presented to the judge based upon your persuasive statements of your experience.

Make sure you avoid a situation in which the judge concludes that your allegations are not truthful (as opposed to the evidence being insufficient), as that conclusion regarding your credibility could harm your divorce case on other issues such as custody and visitation.

6.11   My spouse has threatened to take our child. What should I do to make sure my child is not abducted?

Talk to your lawyer to assess the risks in your particular case. Together you can determine whether statements by your spouse are threats intended to control or intimidate you, or whether legal action is needed to protect your child.

6.12 What legal steps can be taken to prevent my spouse from removing our child from the state?

If you are concerned about your child being removed from the state, ask your lawyer whether any of these options might be available in your case:

- A court order giving you immediate custody until a temporary custody hearing can be held
- A court order directing your spouse to turn over passports for the child and your spouse to the court
- The posting of a bond prior to your spouse exercising parenting time
- Supervised visitation

Both state and federal laws are designed to provide protection from the removal of children from one state to another when a custody matter is brought, and to protect children from kidnapping. *The Uniform Child Custody Jurisdiction and Enforcement Act (UCCJEA)* was passed to ensure that the custody of children is decided in the state where they have been living most recently and where they have the strongest ties. *The Parental Kidnapping Prevention Act (PKPA)* makes it a federal crime for a parent to kidnap a child in violation of a valid custody order.

If you are concerned about your child being abducted, talk with your lawyer about all options available to you for your child's protection. Be proactive on this issue if there is any chance the other parent will try to take your child abroad. *The Hague Convention of 25 October 1980 on the Civil Aspects of International Child Abduction* is an international treaty that may be of assistance in having a child returned. But some countries are not signatories (Japan and most Middle Eastern countries, for example) and some countries that have signed the treaty do not fully enforce its terms (including Brazil and Sweden). Accordingly, focus carefully on prevention. Consult with a divorce attorney capable of advising you on this specific issue.

7

Grounds for Divorce

Marriage in America is a legal status recognized by the state. To end a marriage, a divorce lawsuit must be filed, and a divorce order must be signed by a judge. This chapter addresses many questions you may have regarding your divorce.

7.1   What is a *ground* for divorce?

The *ground* for divorce is the legal basis for the divorce. Virginia law provides for both no-fault and fault grounds of divorce.

7.2   Is Virginia a *no-fault* state?

Yes, spouses may divorce in Virginia without having to prove that the other spouse is guilty of fault. Parties may be granted a divorce once they have lived separately, without cohabitation, for at least one year, provided that at least one of the parties has had the intent to end the marriage for at least one year. The one-year waiting period is shortened to six months if the parties have no minor children, and if they have a written agreement resolving all issues associated with the divorce.

7.3   What are fault grounds for divorce?

The primary fault grounds are adultery, desertion, and cruelty. Sodomy and buggery, though listed, are rarely used in practice. If your spouse is convicted of a felony and sent to prison for at least one year, that provides the basis for a fault-based divorce. There is no waiting period for a divorce based upon adultery; the other fault-based divorces have a one-year waiting period.

7.4   I don't want to sue my spouse for divorce. Is there some other way to get a divorce?

No, the only way to get a divorce is to file a complaint for divorce with the appropriate circuit court clerk. Filing the complaint begins the lawsuit that will result in a judge signing a divorce order. The divorce is granted when the judge signs the divorce order.

7.5   Do I have to be separated for a period of time before I can file for divorce?

Yes. The standard waiting period in Virginia is one year. You may file for divorce based upon adultery with no waiting period, or you can file for a no-fault divorce after a six-month period of separation if you have no minor children, and if you have a written agreement resolving all issues associated with the divorce.

7.6   Do I have to file anything to prove that I am separated?

No, you are separated once you stop living together as a married couple, and at least one of you has the intent to end the marriage. You will need a witness (not your spouse) to testify or to sign an affidavit confirming your separation.

7.7   Do I have to move to prove that I am separated?

Not necessarily. An in-house separation may be sufficient. Either you or your spouse has to have the intent to end the marriage. In addition, you must be separated so you will no longer sleep together, have sex, attend social functions together, or present yourself as a married couple. Your attorney can give you more detailed instructions. You will need a witness (not your spouse) to confirm your separation.

7.8   Do my spouse and I both have to live in Virginia in order to be divorced in Virginia?

No, but at least one of you has to have been a resident of Virginia for at least six months before the divorce complaint is filed.

7.9   I lived in New York with my spouse before I moved here alone. Can I get divorced in Virginia?

Yes, you can seek a divorce in Virginia once you have lived here as a resident for at least six months. But if you have children or property in New York, you should consider seeking a divorce there. If your spouse has remained in New York with your children, Virginia may not have jurisdiction over the property division, custody, visitation, or support.

7.10   Can I file for divorce while I am in bankruptcy?

Yes, but you should consult with a divorce attorney and a bankruptcy lawyer in advance to determine the timing of your bankruptcy and your divorce.

7.11   I have only been married a year. Is an annulment an option for me?

Probably not. Annulments are allowed only under certain specific circumstances including no marriage license, bigamy, incest, impotency, conviction of a felony prior to the marriage, pregnancy on the wife's part by another man, a child fathered by the husband born to another woman within ten months after the marriage, or if either party had been a prostitute. This is just a brief summary of the detailed provisions of the Virginia Code governing annulments that contain exceptions and qualifiers. Even if you have a basis for an annulment, a no-fault divorce would be easier and less expensive to obtain.

7.12   My spouse has told me that she will never give me a divorce. Can I get one in Virginia anyway?

Yes, you will be able to obtain a divorce even if your spouse opposes the divorce.

7.13 How long do I have to have lived in Virginia to get a divorce in the state?

Either you or your spouse has to have been a *bona fide* resident of and domiciled in Virginia for at least six months before the filing of the divorce complaint. This requirement is independent of the waiting period described in this chapter.

7.14 My spouse and I live in different counties in Virginia. Where do I file for divorce?

The preferred venue is either where you last lived together as husband and wife, or where the defendant lives. (The spouse filing suit is the *plaintiff,* and the other spouse is the *defendant.*)

7.15 I am not a citizen of the United States. Can I still get divorced?

Yes, if the other requirements are met. There is no citizenship requirement associated with obtaining a divorce in Virginia.

7.16 Is there a waiting period for a divorce in Virginia?

Yes, for all grounds for divorce except adultery. The standard waiting period is a one-year separation before a complaint for divorce can be filed. If you and your spouse have settled all issues with a written agreement, and if you have no minor children, then the waiting period is six months.

7.17 Is there a way to avoid having the sheriff serve my spouse with divorce papers?

Yes, it is common to cooperate in order to avoid having the sheriff serve the defendant with divorce papers. Instruct your divorce attorney regarding your preferences, and he or she will coordinate with the opposing attorney.

8

Division of Assets and Debts

You and your spouse have assets and debts, some from before the marriage possibly, and some obtained or incurred during the marriage. How are those assets and debts divided and allocated in the divorce? This chapter will address many of your questions by explaining what would happen if your property and debts are allocated and divided by a judge at trial.

Realize, however, that you and your spouse are free to agree upon how to handle the division and allocation of your assets and debts. If you agree, a trial on these issues is not necessary, and the judge will simply accept your agreement. It is very important to become educated regarding your property issues before you begin to negotiate with your spouse.

8.1   Is Virginia a *community property* state?

No, Virginia is an equitable distribution state.

8.2   What does *equitable distribution* mean?

Virginia has an *equitable distribution* system for dividing the assets and debts (for cases in which the parties are unable to resolve the division of assets and debts by agreement). The judge allocates the assets and debts after considering the evidence presented at trial. Though an equal division is common, the judge may divide the assets and debts unequally.

8.3   What is meant by *marital property, separate property,* and *hybrid property*?
If your case goes to trial, the judge is required to "classify" each asset and debt. The *marital property* category includes all property obtained during the marriage by the efforts of one or both of the parties. The *separate property* category includes assets owned or obtained by one of the parties before the marriage, after the parties separated, or during the marriage by gift (not from the other spouse) or inheritance. The *hybrid,* or *part-marital, part-separate* category includes property that has both marital and separate elements. For example, a house purchased with one spouse's inheritance as the down payment, with a mortgage that is paid during the marriage with the parties' earnings is a hybrid asset.

8.4   What is the significance of property classification?
If your case goes to trial, the judge can only divide and allocate marital (and the marital share of hybrid) property. Each party keeps his or her own separate property. The issue of classification is one of the biggest issues in some cases.

8.5   What are the *equitable distribution statutory factors*?
The *equitable distribution statutory factors* identify the evidence that the judge will receive at trial and will consider in making his or her equitable distribution ruling. Your attorney will review these factors with you, and discuss how they apply to the evidence in your case. In many, if not most, cases the parties' assets and debts are equally divided. In some cases, based upon the evidence presented, one party will receive a greater share of the assets or the debt. The equitable distribution statuary factors are listed in the Appendix.

8.6   How is it determined who gets the house?
The house is awarded to the spouse that has the house titled in his or her name. If the house is jointly titled, and the parties cannot agree, then the judge will allocate it based upon what makes the most sense. For example, are the mother and the children currently living in the house? Is the house built on land gifted from the husband's family, and surrounded by the husband's parents and siblings? The party receiving the

house has to be able to refinance the mortgage to end the other spouse's obligation for the mortgage. Which party can afford to do this?

8.7   How do I determine how much our house is worth?

Start with the real estate tax assessment provided by your locality. A realtor can provide additional information. If you need to present a value for trial, you or your attorney will have to arrange for a real estate appraisal by a licensed real estate appraiser.

8.8   My house is worth less than what is owed. What are my options?

The exact solution will depend on whether either you or your spouse is interested in receiving the house subject to the debt. If neither of you wants the house, then it will have to be sold. A normal sale will require that you and your spouse pay the mortgage in full at closing, so you will have to be willing and able to come up with the difference between the sales proceeds (after the realtor's commission, if any) and the mortgage payoff. If you and your spouse are unable or unwilling to come up with that amount of money, then you should discuss with your attorney the possibility of a "short sale," where the lender accepts less money for your house than you owe. The final and least desirable option is a foreclosure. You should discuss these options in detail with your attorney.

8.9   What is meant by *equity* in my home?

The *equity* in your home is the value of the house less the mortgage balance(s).

8.10   How will the equity in our house be divided?

If your home is going to be sold, the equity in the home will most likely be divided at the time of the sale, after the mortgage and costs of the sale have been paid.

If either you or your spouse will be awarded the house, there are a number of options for the other party being compensated for his or her share of the equity in the marital home.

These could include:

- The spouse who does not receive the house receives other assets (for example, retirement funds) to compensate for his or her respective share of the equity.
- The person who remains in the home agrees to refinance the home and to pay the other party his or her share of the equity.
- The parties agree that the property be sold at a future date, or upon the happening of a certain event such as the youngest child completing high school.

As the residence is often among the most valuable assets considered in a divorce, it is important that you and your attorney discuss the details of its disposition. These include:

- valuation of the property
- refinancing to remove a party from liability for the mortgage
- the dates on which certain actions should be taken, such as listing the home for sale
- the real estate agent
- the costs of preparing the home for sale
- making mortgage payments

If you and your spouse do not agree regarding which of you will remain in the home, the court will decide who keeps it or may order the property sold.

8.11 If my spouse signs a quitclaim deed, does that remove his obligation to repay the mortgage?

No, even if you agree to pay the mortgage, his obligation to the mortgage company ends only if you refinance or pay the mortgage in full.

8.12 Who keeps all the household goods until the divorce is final?

The judge rarely makes any rulings regarding the personal property until after the trial, so the parties are usually on their own until then. If you move and take part or even all of the furniture, there is usually nothing the other party can do at that time. On this issue, like most divorce issues, you should try to protect your interests while remaining sensitive to the Golden Rule: If you act in an unfair or overbearing way, you are likely to create additional ill will with the other party, and to invite reciprocal behavior. And you need to remain aware of how your behavior will be viewed by the judge if the case is not settled and goes to trial.

8.13 How can I reduce the risk that assets will be hidden, transferred, or destroyed by my spouse?

Your spouse will be liable if he or she does anything improper with marital assets during the separation. Inventory what you can before the separation, including the contents of your safe deposit box, jewelry, guns, silver, and other collections of value. Prior account statements, loan applications, and financial or net worth statements provide a history of what you and your spouse have owned. Tax returns reflect all accounts that pay interest or dividends. Your divorce attorney can help you with any specific concerns you have.

8.14 When are assets such as cars, boats, and furniture divided?

This can be done at any time by agreement. Otherwise, the judge will handle the division of all assets and debts as part of his or her ruling following trial.

8.15 How do I value our used personal property?

The standard is fair market value: how much the property would sell for if placed on the market. If the property is going to be allocated to one of the parties, the value can be agreed upon. If you can't agree, then an appraiser should be hired if the personal property is of sufficient value to warrant this expense. There are appraisers available to value personal property, guns, jewelry, and coin collections.

8.16 How detailed should my list of assets and debts be?

Your list should include each and every one of the following owned by you, your spouse, or the two of you jointly: real estate, significant items of personal property (cars, boats, and valuable collections), accounts (checking, savings, and stocks), retirement accounts and plans, business interests, other assets of value, mortgages, auto loans, credit card debt, and other debts (not including monthly expenses such as the electric bill).

8.17 What happens to our checking and savings accounts during and after the divorce?

Sometimes a party will take all of the funds from joint accounts. This is an aggressive act that typically guarantees a contentious divorce. The better option in most cases is to act in a thoughtful way with the expectation that the other party will reciprocate. But until you have a clear idea of how the other party is going to behave during the divorce, you do need to be careful to make sure you are not vulnerable. One option is to take one half of the funds from the joint accounts while communicating with the other party to make sure that joint expenses are fairly met. Try to work cooperatively with the other party on these early issues, as that sets the tone for how other issues will be resolved. A hearing can be held before a judge if a conflict develops that cannot be resolved by agreement.

8.18 How and when are liquid assets like bank accounts and stocks divided?

These accounts are often divided early in the process by agreement. If you cannot agree on the division, then the judge will divide and allocate these assets as part of his or her ruling following trial.

8.19 How is pet custody determined?

Virginia does not treat pets as being like children with the need for a custody and visitation ruling. Instead, in divorce cases animals are considered to be personal property to be allocated to one of the parties. In most cases, the spouse that has continued to care for a pet during the separation will be allocated the pet as part of the divorce.

8.20 How will our property in another state be divided?

As a general rule, the same classification and equitable distribution statutory factors apply to property without regard to the location of the property. Talk to your attorney about possible exceptions. For example, contracts and deeds are generally interpreted based upon the law of the jurisdiction in which they were made.

8.21 Are all of the assets—such as property, bank accounts, and inheritances—that I had prior to my marriage still going to be mine after the divorce?

These assets will be classified as your separate property if you kept them separate during the marriage. If you treated an asset as marital, for example by retitling into joint names, then the asset may have become either a marital or a hybrid asset.

If you are unable to agree on this issue, the judge will classify all assets as marital, separate, or hybrid. If these assets are classified as your separate property, then they will be yours after the divorce. The rules governing classification are highly technical, so any specific question you may have will have to be answered by an attorney well versed in Virginia equitable distribution law.

8.22 Will I get to keep my engagement ring?

Yes, if your spouse gave you an engagement ring prior to the marriage, it is your separate property, and your spouse has no claim to it.

8.23 What does it mean to *commingle* property?

Assets with different classifications can be combined (for example, funds held in an account you had before the marriage can be added to a marital checking account), and that combination is referred to as *commingling*. The question then is how is the commingled account classified? The answer to this question depends upon the application of highly technical classification rules to the exact facts of your case.

8.24 Can I keep gifts and inheritances received during the marriage?

This is another classification question. You will be able to keep gifts (not including those from your spouse) and inheritances received during the marriage if you maintained those assets as your separate property during the marriage.

8.25 If my spouse and I can't decide who gets what, who decides?

The judge decides following a trial.

8.26 How are the values of property determined?

Ideally, you and your spouse agree upon the value of property. If you can't agree, then typically an appraisal is obtained if warranted by the value of the asset in dispute. Any unresolved disputes are determined by the judge following a trial.

8.27 What does "date of valuation" mean?

There is typically a one- to two-year gap from the date of separation until the divorce trial (for those cases that are not settled). During that time, some assets change in value. Virginia law requires the judge to use the value at the time of trial, or as close to trial as possible. An exception would be if one of you wasted assets during the separation. In that situation, the judge can select another date as the date of valuation.

8.28 If we agree to, or the judge orders, an equal division of our assets, does that mean that each one of our assets has to be divided?

No, typically some assets are allocated to one party or the other, while others, such as liquid accounts, are divided. An equal division simply means that the total marital value of the assets allocated to you, less the debt allocated to you, equals the value of the assets allocated to your spouse, less the debt allocated to him or her. An equal division means that you and your spouse each receives one half of the net marital estate.

8.29 I worked very hard for years to support my family while my spouse completed an advanced degree. Do I have a right to any of my spouse's future earnings?

Not as a matter of equitable distribution, though you may have a right to receive spousal support. Spousal support is discussed in chapter 10.

8.30 My husband and I have owned and run our business together for many years. Can I be forced out of it?

It depends upon how the business is owned. If the business is titled only to your spouse, then yes, you can be forced out. You will receive some credit for the value of the business, perhaps 50 percent. If it is titled only to you, then you cannot be forced out. If you and your spouse own the business jointly, then the court can order that one of you buy out the other. This is a complicated issue requiring legal advice based upon the specific facts of your case.

8.31 I suspect my spouse is hiding assets, but I can't prove it. How can I protect myself if I discover later that I was right?

If you settle your case, make sure your settlement agreement:

- requires full disclosure
- identifies exactly what assets have been disclosed
- specifies that you receive one half of any subsequently discovered marital assets

8.32 My spouse says I'm not entitled to a share of his stock options because he gets to keep them only if he stays employed with his company. What are my rights?

As a general rule, stock options are marital if they were earned during the marriage, but prior to the separation date. If they are marital, the judge can allocate a percentage of the value of the stock options to you. This can be a complicated issue requiring specific legal advice.

8.33 Will debts be considered when determining the division of the property?

Yes, specific debts are typically allocated with the related asset, if any. For example, if you receive a car, you will almost certainly be responsible for any debt secured by the car. In a more general way, the debts are considered in making the allocation between the parties. For an equal division, your assets less your debts will equal your spouse's assets less his debts.

8.34 What is a *property settlement agreement*?

A *property settlement agreement* between two divorcing spouses typically addresses most, if not all, of the issues in the divorce, including how the parties' assets and debts are to be allocated and divided.

8.35 What happens after my spouse and I sign the property settlement agreement? Do we still have to go to court?

No, you have to go to court only if there are unresolved issues to be determined by the judge. You will still need a divorce order signed by the judge in order to complete the process and obtain your divorce, but that rarely requires a hearing.

8.36 If my spouse and I think our property settlement agreement is fair, does the judge have to approve it?

The judge cannot change your agreement regarding the division of assets and debts, or spousal support, so his or her approval is not required on those issues. The judge does have the power to reject or modify, after a hearing, any settlement terms regarding your minor children, though in practice it is relatively rare for a judge to not accept the terms negotiated by the parents.

8.37 My spouse and I have agreed on how to divide our property. What do we do now?

You should have an attorney assist you in preparing a settlement agreement to be signed by both of you. An oral agreement between you is not enforceable. After your settlement agreement has been signed by both of you, your attorney will assist you in obtaining a no-fault divorce.

8.38 My spouse is guilty of adultery. Does that mean that he will receive less of the property?

It depends upon whether the adultery was pre- or post-separation, other relevant facts, and the judge. Talk to your attorney about this question.

8.39 What, if anything, should I be doing with the credit card companies as we go through the divorce?

As a general rule it is a good idea to close joint credit cards. You will be unable to close accounts with unpaid balances. In that case you should consider sending a letter to the credit card company advising it that you do not agree to be responsible for any future charges. Keep a file copy of your letter.

8.40 How is the credit card debt divided?

The credit card debt is usually allocated as part of an overall settlement of assets and debts. If you and your spouse cannot agree, then this issue is determined by the judge after trial as part of his or her equitable distribution ruling.

8.41 Am I responsible for repayment of my spouse's student loans?

No, probably not.

8.42 During the divorce proceedings, am I still responsible for debt my spouse continues to accrue?

Potentially yes, but usually not.

8.43 During the marriage my spouse applied for and received several credit cards without my knowledge. Am I responsible for them?

You are not responsible to the credit card company unless you signed an application or other document in which you accepted responsibility. The judge has authority as part of equitable distribution to allocate debt to you, even if it was incurred without your knowledge. An important issue would be what the debt was for (for example, credit card debt incurred to buy food for the children would likely be treated differently than debt for entertainment or dating).

8.44 My spouse and I have agreed that I will keep our home; why must I refinance the mortgage?

You must refinance the home because if you didn't, your spouse would remain liable for that debt. The debt would then show on his credit report if he later applies for a mortgage loan, and his credit rating would suffer if you ever became delinquent with your payments.

8.45 Can I file for bankruptcy while my divorce is pending?
You can, but be very careful to make sure that filing for bankruptcy protection is your best option and the timing is appropriate.

You should receive advice from both your bankruptcy and your divorce attorneys before taking this step, as there are usually better options.

9

Retirement and Other Benefits

What impact does the divorce have on your and your spouse's retirement benefits? What happens regarding health insurance coverage? In this area of your divorce, you and your spouse have some flexibility to make arrangements by agreement, but your flexibility is limited by strict state and federal rules.

9.1 Am I entitled to a share of my spouse's retirement benefits?

Just like any other asset, the first issue is classification. You may be entitled to up to one half of the marital share of your spouse's retirement benefits.

9.2 How do I know what part of my spouse's retirement benefits are marital?

The retirement contributions and benefits you and your spouse earned during the marriage (from the date of marriage until the date of the final separation), and the gains and losses on those contributions and benefits, are marital property.

9.3 How much of my retirement account is my spouse able to get as part of our divorce?

Your spouse may be awarded up to, but no more than, 50 percent of the marital share of your retirement account or other retirement benefits. The exact percentage awarded depends upon the specific facts of your case. (*See* equitable distribution statutory factors in the Appendix for the relevant facts to be considered by the judge.) You and your spouse may agree for her to receive more than one half of your retirement accounts. The one-half limitation applies to the judge's authority in the absence of an agreement.

9.4   What is a *qualified domestic relations order?*

A *qualified domestic relations order*, referred to as a *QDRO*, is a special type of order required by federal law to divide a qualified retirement account or plan as part of a divorce.

9.5   If I receive part of my spouse's 401(k) account, when and how will that be done?

A qualified domestic relations order (QDRO) will be entered transferring your share into an account in your name and under your control. This is usually done in conjunction with the entry of the divorce order. Don't delay having the QDRO entered because you could encounter problems if your spouse dies after the divorce order is entered, but before the QDRO is entered.

9.6   How many years must I have been married before I'm eligible to receive a part of my spouse's retirement fund or pension?

There is no required minimum period of marriage under Virginia law, though there is a ten years of marriage requirement to receive a portion of your spouse's military pension.

9.7   My spouse and I have agreed that she will receive one half of my IRA account. When and how will that be done?

Your spouse will receive one half of your IRA account by a rollover of his or her one half into an IRA in his or her name. Typically the investment company that holds the IRA account will need to receive a copy of your divorce settlement agreement specifying the amount or percentage to be transferred to your spouse, a copy of the divorce order, and completed paperwork required by the investment company.

9.8   If I am awarded part of my spouse's retirement benefits, when am I eligible to begin collecting them? Do I have to be sixty-five to collect them?

It depends upon the terms of the plan and federal law. Your attorney can review the retirement plan documentation and provide you with answers to your questions.

9.9   Am I entitled to cost-of-living increases on my share of my spouse's retirement?

You are entitled only if his retirement plan provides for cost-of-living increases, and the order dividing the retirement provides that you share that benefit.

9.10   Does the death of my spouse affect the pay out of retirement benefits to me?

This is an important issue to discuss with your attorney. A simple answer is not possible as so many plan options exist. Be aware of two points. First, have the order dividing the retirement account entered at the time the divorce order is entered to avoid a situation in which your spouse dies after the divorce, but before the retirement account is divided. Second, make sure that you understand in advance any survivor benefit component of the retirement plan, and that the settlement agreement and order dividing the retirement account addresses that issue favorably for you.

9.11   Will I be able to collect on my former spouse's Social Security benefits if he passes on before I do?

If you were married to your spouse for ten or more years and you have not remarried, you may be eligible. Visit your local Social Security Administration office or visit its website at www.ssa.gov.

9.12   What orders might the judge enter regarding life insurance?

The court may require you or your spouse to maintain an existing life insurance policy on one or both of your lives and to designate your children as the beneficiaries. The court can order you to maintain the policy for as long as you have a legal duty to pay child support for your children.

9.13 Because we have young children, should I maintain my ex-spouse as the beneficiary on my life insurance?

You should talk to your attorney about your options. If your spouse is listed as the beneficiary, he or she would have no obligation to use the funds for the benefit of the children. You might consider creating a trust for the benefit of the children, and listing the trust as the beneficiary. You could have your former spouse, or some other trusted person, serve as the trustee. And there are other options.

9.14 Can the judge require in the decree that I be the beneficiary of my spouse's insurance policy, so long as the children are minors, or indefinitely?

Unless you and your spouse agree, the judge cannot require your spouse to designate you as the beneficiary of his or her life insurance policy, regardless of the age of your children.

9.15 My spouse is in the military. What are my rights to his retirement benefits after the divorce?

Your rights depend upon how long you were married, how long your spouse was in the military, how long your spouse was in the military while married to you, and whether you have remarried. This is a complicated area, and rights can be lost if proper procedures are not followed pursuant to strict deadlines. Make sure your attorney has experience with military retirement benefits. If not, he or she should consult with counsel that does have experience in this area.

9.16 I contributed to my pension plan for ten years before I got married. Will my spouse get half of my entire pension?

No, your spouse is not entitled to any part of your pension or retirement benefits earned before the marriage.

9.17   I plan to keep my same job after my divorce. Will my former spouse get half of the money I contribute to my retirement plan after my divorce?

No, only the retirement contributions and benefits earned during the marriage, and the gains and losses on those contributions and benefits, can be divided as part of the divorce.

9.18   Am I still entitled to a share of my spouse's retirement even though I never contributed to one during our marriage?

The judge has authority to award you up to 50 percent of the marital share of your spouse's retirement account. The exact amount awarded to you, if any, will depend upon the facts of your case. The fact that you do not have a retirement account does not disqualify you from receiving up to one half of the marital share of your spouse's retirement accounts or benefits.

9.19   Will I continue to have health insurance through my spouse's work after the divorce?

No, you will no longer be eligible after the divorce, though you may have a COBRA option for a period of time. *COBRA* refers to health insurance benefit provisions provided by a federal statute, the *Consolidated Omnibus Budget Reconciliation Act.*

9.20   What health insurance plans are subject to COBRA?

Group health plans for employers with twenty or more employees are subject to COBRA.

9.21   How do I become eligible for COBRA coverage?

You must be enrolled in a group health plan covered by COBRA on the day before the divorce order is entered by the judge.

9.22   How will I know if I am eligible for COBRA coverage upon divorce?

When you are no longer eligible for health coverage, your spouse's employer will provide you with an election notice, generally within fourteen days, of your right to elect COBRA coverage. If you have questions about your eligibility or rights under *ERISA (Employment Retirement Income Security Act)*, you can call the plan administrator or the Employee Benefit Security Administration (EBSA) toll-free number (866) 444-3272).

9.23 How do I elect COBRA coverage?
You must notify the health insurance plan administrator of your divorce within sixty days. Once the plan administrator receives notice of the divorce, he or she is required to send you an election notice, generally not later than fourteen days after receiving notice of the divorce. You have sixty days after written notice is sent from the plan administrator or health coverage ceased, whichever is later, to elect COBRA coverage.

9.24 When will my COBRA coverage begin?
In the case of divorce, coverage will start on the date of the divorce.

9.25 How long does COBRA coverage last?
COBRA coverage lasts a maximum of thirty-six months.

9.26 What type of health coverage will I receive under COBRA?
Generally, you will have the same coverage you had immediately prior to the divorce. Providers must offer COBRA beneficiaries the same coverage as non-COBRA beneficiaries. A change in benefits for active beneficiaries will also apply to your plan. You will be allowed to make the same choices given to non-COBRA beneficiaries, such as participating in periods of open enrollment offered by the plan.

9.27 How much will COBRA coverage cost?
A COBRA premium cannot exceed 102 percent of the cost of the plan to non-COBRA beneficiaries. Since employers generally pay a portion of health insurance premiums for employees, the cost of COBRA coverage will likely exceed the cost paid for your plan prior to divorce, since you will be responsible for the entire premium. Some employers subsidize COBRA coverage, but they are not required to do so.

9.28   Is COBRA coverage right for me?

If you are in the process of divorce and you are currently covered by health insurance provided by your spouse's employer, you will need to plan for your health insurance coverage upon divorce. You should investigate the cost and coverage of individual plans, any group plans that may be available to you, and plans available through the health insurance marketplace set up as part of the *Affordable Care Act (ACH)* (visit healthcare.gov for more information). As you consider your options, keep in mind the sixty-day deadline for electing COBRA coverage. Whether you choose a COBRA or non-COBRA plan, aim to select a plan that fits within your budget, and provides you with health care coverage that meets your needs.

10

Spousal Support

In Virginia, *spousal support* is the term used to refer to alimony. Most of the questions below will be answered based upon the assumption that you and your spouse are unable to agree and the judge rules on the issue of spousal support. Realize that you and your spouse can agree upon any spousal support arrangement you wish. If you agree upon spousal support, then the judge will not hear evidence and will not make a spousal support ruling. Instead, the judge is required to accept the agreement reached by you and your spouse.

10.1 Which gets calculated first, child support or spousal support?

Spousal support.

10.2 How will I know if I am eligible to receive spousal support?

Adultery, desertion, or other fault on your part may make you ineligible for spousal support. Talk to your attorney about the law and the facts of your case. Review the spousal support statutory factors listed in the Appendix. Those factors identify the evidence the judge would consider if you request spousal support in your divorce case.

10.3 What information should I provide to my attorney if I want spousal support?

All information relevant to any fault in the marriage (adultery or desertion are examples), and relevant to the spousal support statutory factors listed in the Appendix.

10.4 Is there a formula used to determine spousal support in Virginia?

There is a formula, but it applies only for temporary spousal support in the juvenile courts. Otherwise, there is no formula.

10.5 How would the judge decide how much spousal support to award in my case?

The judge would consider all evidence presented by you and your spouse relevant to the spousal support statutory factors and then make a ruling. Because a formula is not used, the decision has an element of subjectivity, which makes predictions difficult.

10.6 How is spousal support paid?

The judge can order monthly support, and/or a lump sum payment.

10.7 If spousal support is awarded on a monthly basis, how long does it continue?

The judge has the authority to award monthly support with or without an ending date.

10.8 If I am ordered to pay spousal support monthly with no ending date, is that permanent?

Your spousal support would end upon your death, your ex-spouse's death, her remarriage, or if you could prove that she has cohabited in a relationship analogous to marriage for at least one year. In addition, the support can be modified or terminated upon a material change in circumstances. For example, the support could be reduced if you suffered a significant reduction in income due to no fault of your own.

10.9   Can I return to court to modify spousal support?

Yes, monthly support ordered by a judge may be modified if there has been a material change in circumstances. Modification is not allowed if you and your spouse agreed upon a specific spousal support arrangement that does not include modification as an option.

10.10   What is a *material change in circumstance?*

For purposes of modifying spousal support, a *material change in circumstances* is almost always a significant, unforeseen change in one or both of the parties' earning capacity or expenses. A material change in circumstances has to be present for the judge to be able to modify spousal support.

10.11   Can I reduce my spousal support obligation by changing to a lower-paying job?

No, you cannot intentionally create a material change in circumstances to reduce your support. In any event, spousal support is based upon your earning capacity, even if you choose to work at a lower-paying job.

10.12   My spouse makes a lot more money than I do. Will I be awarded spousal support to make up the difference in our income?

There is no requirement that spousal support be used to equalize incomes postdivorce. That is not the goal or purpose of spousal support.

10.13   My spouse makes a lot more money than is reported on our tax return. How can I prove my spouse's real income to show he can afford to pay spousal support?

You will need the help of your attorney and possibly also the help of an accountant. There are many ways to hide income. Your attorney can assist you in obtaining all relevant records, and in building the case to show the judge that your spouse's real income is higher than his reported income.

10.14. I want to be sure the records on the spousal support I pay are accurate, especially for tax purposes. What's the best way to ensure this?

Don't pay cash. Either write and send monthly checks with "spousal support" noted on the memo line or arrange for a monthly electronic transfer of the spousal support payments.

10.15 What effect does spousal support have on my taxes?

Unless you and your spouse agree otherwise, and subject to certain exceptions and limitations, spousal support is deductible to the party paying and taxable to the party receiving the support. For example, for a $500 per month spousal support obligation, the annual taxable income of the party paying the support is reduced by $6,000 and the annual taxable income of the party receiving the support is increased by $6,000.

10.16 Can I continue to collect spousal support if I move to a different state?

Yes, the court order providing for spousal support stays in effect even if you move from Virginia.

10.17 Does remarriage affect my spousal support?

Yes, remarriage terminates your spousal support under Virginia law. (There is an exception if you have a written agreement, incorporated in a court order, that specifically provides that spousal support continues after you remarry.)

10.18 Does the death of my former spouse affect my spousal support?

Yes, spousal support terminates upon your death or your ex-spouse's death.

10.19 I started an affair before my spouse and I separated. How will that impact my claim for spousal support?

It is possible that your claim for spousal support will be barred by your adultery. Whether your spousal support claim is barred due to your adultery depends upon whether your spouse is also guilty of adultery or other fault, on how your financial situation compares with your spouse's, and how your misbehavior compares with your spouse's marital misbehavior.

10.20 Do I have to keep paying spousal support if my former spouse is now living with a new significant other?

If your spousal support is based upon an agreement, then it depends upon the terms of the agreement. If your spousal support obligation is based upon a ruling by the judge, then your obligation continues until you can prove that your ex-spouse has been living with another person for at least a year in a relationship analogous to marriage.

10.21 My spouse and I have only been married for four years. How will that impact my claim for spousal support?

The duration of the marriage is one of the spousal support statutory factors. Generally speaking, if spousal support is ordered, then it would typically be for a shorter duration than it would be for a longer marriage.

10.22 My husband says that he is going to quit his job so that he does not have to pay me spousal support. Can he do that?

His strategy would almost certainly be unsuccessful. As required by the spousal support statutory factors, the judge would consider not only his income, but also his earning capacity. The judge would likely impute income to your husband if he quit his job to avoid paying you support.

10.23 What does it mean to *impute* income?

If a spouse's income is less than his or her earning capacity (that is, if he or she is unemployed or underemployed), the judge has the authority to consider his or her earning capacity in making the spousal support ruling. Income is *imputed* when the judge finds that a party has an earning capacity higher than his or her income, and bases the spousal support ruling on that earning capacity.

10.24 What happens if my former spouse does not pay his spousal support obligation?

You have a range of enforcement options. You can contact the Division of Child Support Enforcement if your ex-spouse also owes you child support; you can file a show cause for contempt action to have the judge force payment under penalty of punishment, including jail; your ex-spouse can have his bank accounts and his tax refunds garnished; and he can lose his driver's license.

10.25 If I am awarded spousal support in my divorce, can this obligation be discharged if my former spouse files for bankruptcy after our divorce?

No.

10.26 If I have to pay monthly spousal support with no ending date, does that mean I can never retire?

That is a problem. In some cases retirement is treated as material change of circumstances and the judge reduces or terminates the spousal support obligation. In other cases the spousal support is not reduced or modified based upon a party's retirement. Because of this uncertainty, it is preferable to reach an agreement with your spouse regarding spousal support that takes retirement into account.

10.27 I was divorced last year and did not request spousal support. Can I go back to court now and get spousal support?

No, unless the divorce order contains a reservation of support.

10.28 What is a *reservation of spousal support*?

A *reservation of spousal support* is a sentence in the divorce order that reserves jurisdiction for the judge to make a spousal support ruling in the future. Without this sentence in the divorce order, spousal support cannot be ordered in the future. The reservation is for a specific period of time. Once that time has elapsed, the judge cannot order spousal support. Any party that is free of fault with regard to the marriage can request and receive a reservation of spousal support. The reservation is usually for one half the length of the marriage.

11

Custody and Visitation

Custody and visitation are often the most emotional issues to be addressed in a divorce. With rare exceptions, both parents love their child or children and are very concerned with preserving or improving their relationship with their child during and following the divorce. Before the divorce, both parents typically spend time daily with their child. Once the parties separate, both parties have to accept a schedule in which they do not necessarily see their child on a daily basis. This is often hard to accept.

Because in most cases both parties would like to see their child daily, it is easy to see the custody and visitation issues as a competitive situation in which each party tries to maximize his or her time with the child, and there is a winner (the parent with the most time) and a loser (the visiting parent). Both parents should strive to avoid this competitive, win-lose framework.

It is very important to keep in mind the child's perspective and his or her best interests. Your child loves both of his or her parents, and needs a healthy relationship with both. Though it is hard, make every effort to do what is best for your child, even if that means a schedule or arrangement that is not your preference.

There are many studies, some conflicting, with regard to the effect of divorce on the healthy development of children. On one issue there seems to be agreement: high levels of conflict between his or her parents is not in a child's best interests. As you work through the issues of custody and visitation and the other divorce issues, make your best effort to be nice and fair to your spouse. Be cooperative with the hope that your spouse will reciprocate. Do it for your child or children.

11.1   What does *physical custody* mean?

Physical custody refers to the day-to-day care of and responsibility for the child. Physical custody can be primary with one parent, or shared.

11.2   What does *legal custody* refer to?

Legal custody refers to the decision-making authority with regard to important decisions affecting the child, such as the choice of school, the choice of health care providers, and specific nonroutine decisions such as whether to prescribe medication to help address a child's behavioral problems.

One parent can have *sole legal custody,* or the parents can share *joint legal custody.* Joint legal custody is often considered best for the child, but only if the parents are capable of acting in a cooperative manner in the child's best interests.

11.3   On what basis will the judge award custody?

The judge will award custody only if you and your spouse cannot agree regarding the custody and visitation arrangements. If you cannot agree and have to go to court, the judge will consider evidence relevant to the custody and visitation statutory factors, which are listed in the Appendix. The standard in Virginia is the best interests of the child. The judge is required to make a ruling that is in the child's best interests. The judge has considerable discretion as this determination has an unavoidably subjective element.

11.4   In the context of my divorce, what does *visitation* mean?

Visitation refers to the schedule that one or both of the parents (usually the parent that has less time with the children) has with the children.

11.5 Is there a way for my spouse and me to agree upon custody and visitation without having to go to court?

As with all of your divorce issues, you should seek a compromise settlement of the custody and visitation issues. You should communicate and resolve your differences directly with your spouse, if possible. Alternatively, the attorneys can negotiate on your behalf. Mediation or collaborative law works for some parents. Mediation with a child psychologist is sometimes effective in reaching an agreement. *See* chapter 15 for an additional discussion of settlement issues.

11.6 What options do my spouse and I have regarding our child's schedule once we separate?

There are numerous schedule options, including an alternating week with each parent; Monday and Tuesday with one parent, Wednesday and Thursday with the other parent, and alternating weekends; and one night during the week and every other weekend visitation for one parent with the other parent having custody the remaining times. There are many other possible schedules, and holidays and summers also have to be addressed.

11.7 What custody and visitation schedule will the judge order for our children?

The judge will order a schedule for your children only if you and your spouse cannot agree upon a schedule. If necessary, the judge will order a schedule for your children after considering the evidence presented as required by the custody and visitation statutory factors (*see* the Appendix for the custody and visitation statutory factors). The judge is required to make a ruling that, in his or her judgment, serves the best interests of the children. Each family situation is different, so there are a variety of schedules ordered in different cases.

11.8 What is a guardian *ad litem*? Why is one appointed?

A guardian *ad litem,* or *GAL,* is an attorney that is appointed to represent your child in the custody and visitation case. In some courts a GAL is appointed automatically. In most courts a GAL is appointed only if one of the parties files a motion requesting that a GAL be appointed. A judge will appoint a GAL if he or she concludes that the child's best interests require a GAL, and that a GAL would assist the judge in determining the child's best interests.

11.9 Will my children be present if we go to court?

Either parent can bring the children to court, though in most cases the children are not present. If a GAL has been appointed to represent the children, then the issue of bringing the children to court should be discussed with him or her. Children should be shielded as much as possible from the divorce proceedings, and they should be involved in a court case only for compelling reasons.

11.10 How much weight does the child's preference carry?

It depends upon the age and maturity of the child and the judge. The older and more mature the child, the more weight his or her preference carries. For example, the reasonable preference of a seventeen-year-old would typically carry significant weight, while the preference of an eleven-year-old to spend more time with the more fun and easy going parent would not carry much weight.

11.11 How old do the children have to be before they can speak to the judge about where they want to live?

There is no specific age limit requirement. It depends upon the age and maturity of the child and the policy of the judge.

11.12 If my child wants to talk to the judge, does he have to do that in open court in front of both parents and our attorneys?

Typically the child would talk privately with the judge without the parents or the attorneys being present. There are specific rules governing this process that you should discuss with your attorney.

11.13 Will my attorney want to speak to my child?

Not usually, unless he or she is going to call your child as a witness to testify in court.

11.14 Do I have to let my spouse see the children if I don't trust him to return them when he should?

It is important that you act in your children's best interests. With rare exceptions, children benefit from regular contact with both parents. One of the custody and visitation statutory factors is whether either parent has interfered with the other parent's relationship with the children. If your case ends up in court, the judge may hold it against you if you have not allowed your spouse to see the children. Both parents should cooperate to avoid having a tug-of-war with the children. Involve the attorneys, a child psychologist, or a judge, if necessary.

11.15 I am seeing a therapist. Will that hurt my chances of getting custody?

Obtaining help for any mental health issues will almost certainly not be held against you, though the underlying mental health condition may be an issue. For example, if you are a suicidal schizophrenic your chances of getting custody are slight. If you are anxious and depressed associated with the divorce, and you have obtained appropriate treatment, this likely will have little or no effect on your custody case.

11.16 I am taking prescription medication to treat my depression. Will this hurt my chances of getting custody?

The issue is your condition. If your depression is under control with the help of the prescription medication, if there are no side effects that would impact your children, and if you are consistent in meeting with your doctor and taking your medication, then this will likely have little or no effect on your custody case.

11.17 Will the fact that I had an affair during the marriage hurt my chances of getting custody?

It depends upon whether your conduct had any impact on your child, or upon your relationship with your child. It could hurt your chances if you exposed your child to your adulterous relationship, or if you regularly chose to spend time with your paramour rather than your child. Otherwise, the affair should have little impact on your custody case.

11.18 During the months it takes to get a divorce, is it okay to date or would that hurt my custody case?

While you are still married you should not expose your child to your dating relationships. Your custody case should not be harmed if you choose to date while your child is with the other parent (assuming your boyfriend or girlfriend is not a sex offender or other inappropriate choice).

11.19 Can having a live-in partner hurt my chances of getting custody?

Yes, this could hurt your chances. The exact impact will depend upon the specific facts of your case and the preferences of the judge. Some judges add a condition to the custody and visitation order that neither party can have a boyfriend or girlfriend spend the night on the nights when that parent has the children.

11.20 I'm gay and came out to my spouse when I filed for divorce. What impact will my sexual orientation have on my case for custody?

Your sexual orientation should have no impact on your custody and visitation case, though it is possible that there are judges that would hold this against you. Your sexual behavior could impact your case, just as the sexual behavior of a heterosexual can impact his or her case. Judges are concerned that children not be exposed to inappropriate behavior.

11.21 Can I have witnesses speak on my behalf in my custody case?

Yes, though family members and close friends are usually of limited value as it is understood that they love you and want you to obtain the best possible outcome. Non-family members, such as teachers or day care providers, who are not biased towards either party, can be valuable witnesses.

11.22 What is a *child-custody expert*? Why is one appointed?

Either party can file a motion to have a *child-custody expert,* usually a specially trained evaluator (who typically also works as a children's therapist, though not in the same case in which he or she is an evaluator). A party requests the appointment of an expert when he or she thinks the evaluator will bring to the judge's attention negative personality traits or relationship issues of the other party, and positive personality traits or relationship issues involving him or herself. These evaluations are expensive, and in most cases the judge can understand the family situation and dynamics without the need for an expert. Expert evaluations are not used in most cases.

11.23 How might photographs or a video of my child help my custody case?

Scrapbook-type photographs are frequently used, but are usually of limited value. Sometimes photographs or video are used as evidence of physical abuse. You should obtain legal advice in this situation. Sometimes these photographs or videos are held against the parent presenting the evidence on the basis that the taking of the photographs can make the child feel uncomfortably involved in the case. (This is typically not an issue if the child is too young to understand, or if the child is sleeping when the photographs are taken.)

11.24 Does shared physical custody mean equal time at each parent's house?

No, there are many possible shared physical custody schedules. For example, one parent could have three days per week, and the other could have four; one parent could have five or six days every two weeks; or one parent could have most of the summer, the other parent could have most school nights, and the parents could equally share weekend time. The focus should be on creating the best possible schedule for the child, not on making sure that each parent gets exactly one half of the time.

11.25 If I have sole custody, may I move out of state without the judge's permission?

Under Virginia law, every custody and visitation order includes a requirement that you give the other party thirty days' advance notice before you move out of state with your child. If the other parent does not agree to modify the visitation arrangement to accommodate the move, then you will need a hearing to obtain permission of the judge. This answer is the same no matter what custody arrangement you have.

11.26 What does it mean to have *split custody*?

Split custody refers to an arrangement in which each parent has custody of at least one of the children. Though parents and judges typically prefer to have similar schedules for the children, sometimes it makes sense for one parent to have custody of one child while the other parent has custody of the other.

11.27 What is a *parenting plan*?

Parenting plans provide guidance for parents on issues likely to cause conflict between them in the future if not considered. For example, parenting plans may address issues such as decision-making authority, discipline, and the division of parental responsibilities. A parenting plan typically includes custody and visitation arrangements, including details such as scheduling, exchanges, and procedures for resolving scheduling changes or conflicts. A parenting plan may provide guidance on other issues such as communications between the parents, communications between the parents and children, nonparent child care, and dispute resolution.

Virginia law does not require the creation of parenting plans. Nevertheless, parents are free to work together by agreement to create a parenting plan for how they are going to co-parent their children after the divorce. If the parents agree, a parenting plan can be included or incorporated in a custody and visitation order entered by the judge.

Even though Virginia law does not require the creation of parenting plans, many of the issues and details provided for in a parenting plan are included in settlement agreements and in custody and visitation orders.

11.28 If my spouse is awarded legal custody, can I still take my child to church during my parenting time?

Yes, it is highly unlikely that a judge would attempt to restrict your choice of religious activities with your child during your parenting time, absent a clear and serious threat to your child's well-being.

11.29 What if my child does not want to visit her dad? Can he force her to go?

If there is a court-ordered visitation schedule, you are required to obey and respect the schedule. The child's wishes do not trump a court order. If you do not make the child available for visitation, you are in violation of a court order and can be charged with contempt of court. If your child has a good reason, the proper procedure would be to file a motion to modify the visitation.

11.30 What if my child is not returned by her mother at the agreed-upon time? Should I call the police?

Police involvement is stressful for the parents and the children. The police should be called only if necessary for someone's physical safety. Other disputes should be handled between the parents, with the attorneys, and with the judge, if necessary.

Try to have a broad perspective regarding any concern involving your child. Focus on your child's best interests and try to minimize conflict with the other parent. For example, if a child is returned late as an isolated incident, you should do nothing. If the child is returned late as a pattern and as a result doesn't have time to finish his homework, you should communicate with the other parent in a polite manner about your concerns. If the other parent is not responsive to your concerns on any parenting issue, then discuss your concerns with your attorney. If your concerns are serious enough, they can be brought to the judge's attention.

11.31 My spouse argues with me in front of the children and talks to them about the divorce. What should I do?

Avoid arguments and conflict with the other parent in the presence of the children. Shield your children as much as possible from conflict and involvement in the divorce. Things are hard enough for them. Let them be children. You and your spouse are adults and should handle your divorce in a mature, thoughtful way. You both love your children, so do what you can to protect them from the negative emotions and words associated with your divorce.

11.32 I am considering moving out of Virginia. What factors will the court consider in either granting or denying my request to remove my child from Virginia?

The standard for all issues involving your child is his or her best interests. You will be allowed to move your child out of state only if the move is in the child's best interests. In most cases the biggest issue is the child's relationship with the other parent. What impact will the move have on that relationship? The public policy in Virginia is for both parents to have frequent and continuing contact, and to be involved in the child's care and upbringing.

11.33 After the divorce, can my spouse legally take our child out of the state during parenting time? Out of the country?

Absent a specific restriction in the court order, neither parent is limited with regard to travel during his or her time with the child.

11.34 If I am not given custody, what rights do I have regarding school and medical records?

Under Virginia law, both parents have access to their child's academic and medical, hospital, and other health records. This right of access applies to both parents regardless of the specific custody and visitation arrangement.

11.35 Can I attend my child's medical examination scheduled during the other parent's time?

It is important that parents cooperate on things like this for the sake of their child. It is good for the child to have the benefit of both parents' concern and involvement. This should not be a source of conflict between parents, but if it is, consider whether the harm to your child due to the conflict outweighs the benefit to her of both parents attending. If you don't attend, you can talk to the doctor and review the medical records after the appointment.

11.36 What if my child has suffered abuse from the other parent? Do I still have to force my child to continue to visit?

This is a terrible situation to have to deal with. On the one hand you feel you have to do everything you can to keep your child safe, and on the other hand you have to obey all court orders. Obtain legal advice immediately. If there has been abuse, your attorney will help guide you through the process which may include a motion to modify the custody and visitation order, a report to social services, and a criminal complaint. Be very careful. You want to protect your child, but if the judge later concludes that you made serious, unfounded allegations against the other parent, your parenting time could be reduced, and you could even lose custody.

11.37 What does it mean to be an *unfit parent*?

An *unfit parent* is a parent who either engages in misconduct that affects their child, neglects his or her child, or demonstrates an unwillingness or inability to promote the emotional or physical well-being of their child. The home environment and moral climate created by the parent are important factors in determining whether he or she is unfit.

11.38 How can I get my spouse's visitation to be supervised?

Supervised visitation is ordered only when supervision is required for the safety and well-being of the child. A concern that the other parent is not a good parent for one reason or the other is not sufficient. As a general rule, supervised visitation is ordered only when physical or sexual abuse, or neglect by the visiting parent has been proven. Supervised visitation may be ordered during the investigation following an allegation of abuse or neglect.

11.39 I want to talk to my spouse about our child, but all she wants to do is argue. How can I communicate without it always turning into a fight?

Because conflict is high between you and your spouse, consider the following:

• Ask your lawyer to help you obtain a court order for custody and visitation that is specific and detailed.

This lowers the amount of necessary communication between you and your spouse.

- Put as much information as possible in writing.
- Consider using e-mail or texts.
- Avoid criticisms of your spouse's parenting.
- Avoid telling your spouse how to parent.
- Be factual and business-like.
- Acknowledge to your spouse the good parental qualities he or she displays, such as being concerned, attentive, or generous.
- Keep your child out of any conflicts.

By focusing on your own behavior, you may be able to reduce conflict with your spouse. Most of us are critical of others while being reluctant to analyze our own behavior with the same critical eye. Additionally, talk to your attorney about developing a communication protocol to follow when communicating with your spouse.

11.40 What steps can I take to prevent my spouse from getting our child in the event of my death?

The other parent becomes the custodial parent automatically upon your death. One of your friends or family members could seek custody at that time. The law favors the parent, so this contest would be hard for the nonparent to win. As a general rule, for a nonparent to win custody over a parent, the nonparent would have to prove that the parent was unfit or that he or she had abandoned the child.

12

Child Support

Because Virginia has guidelines and a formula, child support is often one of the easier issues in a divorce. This chapter will explain the Virginia child-support guidelines and how child support is calculated in Virginia, and will address the most common questions regarding child support.

12.1 How is child support determined in Virginia?
Child support guidelines are used in determining child support.

12.2 What is a *child-support guidelines work sheet*?
A *child-support guidelines work sheet* is used in Virginia to determine child support according to the child-support guidelines. There are two primary versions of the work sheet:
- one to be used in situations in which one parent has sole physical custody
- one to be used in situations in which the parents have shared physical custody

12.3 How is the *monthly basic child-support obligation* determined?
The *monthly basic child-support obligation* is determined from a schedule in the Virginia Code. The exact amount in your case depends upon the total income of the parents, and the total number of children for whom child support is being paid. The schedule can be reviewed online at Code of Virginia §20-108.2.B. Go to www.vadivorcelaw.net (select) Virgina

Code Sections, then, under Child support—cash medical support (select) Code §20-108.2.B or go to http://leg1.state.va.us/cgi-bin/legp504.exe?000+cod+20-108.2.

12.4 What factors are used to calculate child support?

Several factors are considered in calculating child support. These include:

- both parents' income
- spousal support
- support for other children
- the number of children of the parties
- the cost to provide health insurance coverage for the children
- employment-related child-care expenses
- the number of days the child spends with each parent

12.5 Will the custody and visitation arrangement I have impact the amount of child support I receive?

Yes. If one of the parents has the child less than ninety-one days per year, then the regular child-support guidelines work sheet is used. If both parents have the child for at least ninety-one days per year, then the shared-custody guidelines work sheet is used.

12.6 How are *days* counted?

A *day* is defined as a twenty-four hour period. Overnight but less than twenty-four hours counts as one half day. Time during the day but not overnight does not count towards the day count.

12.7 Is overtime pay considered in the calculation of child support?

Usually, yes, unless it is clear that it is not available going forward.

12.8 Will rental income be factored into my child support, or just my salary?

Your rental income will be included as part of your income for purposes of calculating child support. You can have the gross rental income reduced by proving reasonable and legitimate expenses associated with owning the property.

12.9 What else is included as income for purposes of calculating child support?

For the purposes of calculating child support, *gross income* means all income from all sources including:

- salaries
- wages
- commissions
- royalties
- bonuses
- dividends
- severance pay
- pensions
- interest
- trust income
- annuities
- capital gains
- Social Security benefits (with exceptions)
- workers' compensation benefits
- unemployment insurance benefits
- disability insurance benefits
- veterans' benefits
- spousal support
- rental income
- gifts
- prizes or awards

12.10   My spouse has a college degree but refuses to get a job. Will the judge consider this in determining the amount of child support?

If a parent is underemployed or unemployed, the judge may impute income to that parent. If a judge imputes income to a parent, she is basing the support on that parent's earning capacity rather than actual income. There are specific rules regarding what evidence must be presented before the judge will impute income, so you should discuss this issue with your attorney.

12.11   Is there a way for me to calculate child support without hiring an attorney?

Several websites provide a Virginia child-support calculator, including Raynor Law Office, P.C.: at www.raynorlawoffice. com, go to Resources, Child Support Calculator and www.sup-portsolver.com.

12.12   Can I get temporary support while waiting for custody to be decided?

Yes, there are procedures available to obtain temporary child support. *See* chapter 18.

12.13   How soon does my spouse have to start paying child support for our child?

Your spouse's legal obligation for child support begins once you file a request for child support with an appropriate court.

12.14   Will I get the child support directly from my spouse or from the state?

Either parent can request that child support be paid through the *Division of Child Support Enforcement (DCSE)*. If neither parent requests the involvement of DCSE, then the support will be paid directly from the other parent.

12.15 What are the pros and cons of having the child support paid through DCSE?

The primary benefit of using DCSE is that they will keep records of the payments, and they will take collection action against the party paying support if he or she stops paying. The downside is that DCSE is a governmental bureaucracy, so there are sometimes problems such as delays or communication issues.

12.16 Will some amount of child support be withheld from every paycheck?

The parent receiving child support can request that the support be withheld from the other parent's paycheck. If support is paid by payroll withholding, typically the same amount is withheld each pay period. (To calculate this amount, multiply the monthly child support by 12 and then divide that total by the total number of pay periods per year—usually 12, 24, 26, or 52.)

12.17 The person I am divorcing is not the biological parent of my child. Can I still collect child support from my spouse?

The general rule in Virginia is that a parent only has a duty to support his natural or legally adopted children, not his stepchildren.

12.18 What happens with child support when our child goes to the other parent's home for summer vacation? Is child support still due?

Yes, child support is typically calculated taking into account the child's schedule for the entire year. The child-support amount is then paid each month, even when the child is with the other parent.

12.19 When does child support end?

Child support terminates once the child has 1) reached the age of eighteen, and 2) graduated from high school. Child support terminates at age nineteen even if the child has not graduated from high school.

12.20 Can I expect to continue to receive child support if I remarry?

Yes, your marital status has no impact on child support.

12.21 After the divorce, if I choose to live with my new partner rather than marry, will that affect child support?

No, though there are exceptions. For example, if your new partner gave you a certain sum of money each month, or paid your mortgage or other expenses that could change your income which could affect the child-support amount. This answer applies equally whether you are married to or just live with your new partner.

12.22 Are expenses such as child care supposed to be taken out of my child support?

Work-related child-care expenses are factored into the child-support calculation, and you are then responsible for the payment of your own child-care costs.

12.23 Am I required to pay for all expenses for my child with the child support I receive?

You are responsible for all expenses for your child while he or she is in your care, and the other parent is responsible for the expenses for the child while the child is with him. Uninsured medical expenses for the child are shared by the parents. Expenses such as piano lessons and sports fees can be shared by the parents by agreement, but absent an agreement or specific terms of a court order, neither parent is required to contribute to the costs associated with extracurricular activities.

12.24 Can my spouse be required by the support order to pay for our child's private school?

Yes, the judge has the authority to order the payment of private school tuition, but that liability is not automatic. If you and your spouse cannot agree on whether your child is going to attend private school, or on how the tuition and costs will be paid, talk to your attorney about your options based upon the law and your specific situation.

12.25 Can my spouse be required by court order to contribute financially to our child's college education?

An agreement between you and your spouse for the payment of college education costs for your child is valid, but if you cannot agree, the judge has no authority to require either of you to contribute to your child's college costs.

12.26 What is a *cash medical support order*?

A *cash medical support order* directs you and the other parent to pay (in proportion to your incomes) the reasonable and necessary unreimbursed medical and dental expenses of your children.

12.27 How does providing health insurance for my children affect my child-support amount?

The cost to add the children to your health insurance policy (the difference between the cost for you alone and for you and the children) is included in the child-support calculation.

12.28 Am I required to pay for my child's uninsured medical expenses from the child support I receive?

Each party is required to pay for his or her share of the child's uninsured medical expenses. You can use any source of income you wish to pay your share.

12.29 Will my child continue to have health insurance coverage through my spouse's work even though we're divorcing?

The divorce does not impact a parent's ability to provide health insurance coverage for his or her children.

12.30 After the divorce, can my former spouse substitute buying items directly for our child for child-support payments?

No. If you seek child support through the Division of Child Support Enforcement or the court, then a child-support order will be entered that will have to be complied with. The other parent will have to pay you the child-support amount.

12.31 Can I still collect child support if I move to another state?

Yes.

12.32 I live outside of Virginia. Will the money I spend on airline tickets to see my child impact my child support?

You can ask the judge to take that expense into account. Talk to your attorney about this issue.

12.33 Can the judge enter a child-support amount different from the amount called for by the child-support guidelines work sheet?

Yes, the judge can deviate from the guidelines amount for one of the reasons listed in the Virginia Code. These reasons, commonly referred to as *Child Support Deviation Factors,* are listed in the Appendix.

12.34 Does interest accrue on past-due child support?

Yes, at 6 percent per annum.

12.35 What can I do if my former spouse refuses to pay child support?

You first need to obtain a child-support order. You can then have the Division of Child Support Enforcement collect the support for you, you can file a show cause yourself in the juvenile court, or you can have your attorney help you collect.

12.36 At what point will the Division of Child Support Enforcement help me collect back child support, and what methods do they use?

The DCSE will help you collect child support as soon as an administrative or court order for support is entered.

Upon your request or where a delinquency equal to at least one month of child support exists, the state can issue an order requiring that the parent's employer withhold income to satisfy the child-support obligation.

When past-due support is owed, a lien may be placed on the property or assets may be collected from the delinquent parent's financial accounts.

Within certain limits, unemployment compensation may be intercepted to satisfy a child-support obligation.

Federal and state tax returns also may be intercepted where a delinquency of at least $25 exists.

Under certain circumstances, where an arrears of at least $1,000 for an ongoing support obligation exists ($500 for arrears-only), the property of the parent owing support may be seized and sold.

Where other methods have failed or no other method is feasible and the amount of delinquency exceeds $1,000, bonds, securities, or guarantees may be used to collect back child support.

Driver's licenses, professional licenses, and recreational licenses can be suspended if support payments of $5,000 or more are delinquent for ninety days or more.

Where more than $2,500 is owed, the U.S. Department of State will not issue a U.S. passport. In some cases, failure to pay child support can result in a jail sentence.

You must initiate contact with DCSE if you want help in collecting your child support.

12.37 Can child support be changed?

Yes, if there has been a material change in circumstances. To change or modify child support, there has to have been a significant change affecting your income, the other parent's income, health insurance costs, child-care costs, or the number of children covered by the support order.

12.38 Our son is disabled. Will the other parent have to help support him after he turns eighteen?

That is an option, but it is not automatic. Make sure you obtain legal advice on this point as early as possible, and well in advance of your child's eighteenth birthday. You may be required to seek and obtain a court order prior to your child turning eighteen.

12.39 If I am awarded child support, can this obligation be discharged if my former spouse files for bankruptcy after our divorce?

No.

12.40 My husband pays child support a few days late every month. What can I do about this?

You can seek a *wage withholding order.*

12.41 Can I insist that my ex-wife provide an accounting of how she spends the child support I provide?

No, she does not have to account to you for how she spends the child support.

13

Tax Issues

Nobody likes a surprise letter from the Internal Revenue Service saying he or she owes more taxes. When your divorce is over, you want to be sure that you don't later discover you owe taxes you weren't expecting to pay.

Taxes are an important consideration in both settlement negotiations and trial preparation. They should not be overlooked. Taxes can impact many of your decisions, including those regarding spousal support, equitable distribution, and the receipt of benefits.

The following information is for general educational purposes only. It seems that every IRS rule has numerous, sometimes complicated, exceptions. Do not consider the following to be legal advice. Be sure to obtain tax advice from your divorce attorney, a tax attorney, or a certified public accountant (CPA).

13.1 Will either my spouse or I have to pay income or capital gains tax when we transfer property or pay a property settlement to one another according to our divorce decree?

No. The allocation of assets and debts between spouses as part of a divorce is not taxable. Likewise, the payment from one spouse to another as part of the resolution of the divorce property issues is not taxable. However, it is important that you recognize the future tax consequences of a subsequent withdrawal, sale, or transfer of assets you receive in your divorce. It is important to ask your attorney to take tax consequences into consideration when looking at the division of your assets.

13.2 Is the amount of child support I pay tax deductible?

No.

13.3 Do I have to pay income tax on any child support I receive?

No.

13.4 Is the amount of spousal support I am ordered to pay tax deductible?

Yes, subject to a number of exceptions.

13.5 Do I have to pay tax on the spousal support I receive?

Yes, subject to a number of exceptions. Income tax is a critical factor in determining a fair amount of spousal support. Insist that your attorney bring this issue to the attention of your spouse's lawyer, or to the judge if your case proceeds to trial, so that both the tax you pay and the deduction your spouse receives are taken into consideration.

Be sure to consult with your tax advisor about payment of tax on your spousal support. Making estimated tax payments throughout the year, or withholding additional taxes from your wages can avoid a burdensome tax liability at the end of the year.

It is important to budget for payment of tax on your spousal support. Taxes are also another item to consider when looking at your monthly living expenses for the purposes of seeking a spousal support award.

13.6 What is our tax filing status during the divorce proceedings?

You are considered unmarried if your decree is final by December 31 of the tax year. If you are considered unmarried, your filing status is either "single" or, under certain circumstances, "head of household."

If your decree is not final as of December 31, your filing status is either "married filing a joint return" or "married filing a separate return," unless you meet the requirements for filing as "head of household."

While your divorce is in progress, talk to both your tax advisor and your attorney about your filing status. It may be beneficial to figure your tax on both a joint return and a separate return to see which gives you the lower tax. *IRS Publication 504, Divorced or Separated Individuals,* provides more detail on tax issues while you are going through a divorce.

13.7 Should I file a joint income tax return with my spouse while our divorce is pending?

Consult your tax advisor to determine the risks and benefits of filing a joint return with your spouse. Compare this with the consequences of filing your tax return separately. Often the overall tax liability will be less with the filing of a joint return, but other factors are important to consider.

When deciding whether to file a joint return with your spouse, consider any concerns you have about the accuracy and truthfulness of the information on the tax return. If you have any doubts, consult both your attorney and your tax advisor before agreeing to sign a joint tax return with your spouse. Prior to filing a return with your spouse, try to reach agreement about how any tax owed or refund expected will be shared, and ask your lawyer to assist you in getting this in writing.

13.8 My spouse will not cooperate in providing the necessary documents to prepare or file our taxes jointly. What options do I have?

You will have to file married filing separately unless you meet the requirements for filing as head of household.

13.9 For tax purposes, is one time of year better than another to divorce?

It depends upon your tax situation. If you and your spouse agree that it would be beneficial to file joint tax returns, you may wish to not have your divorce finalized before the end of the year.

Your marital status for filing income taxes is determined by your status on December 31. If you both want to preserve your right to file a joint return, your decree should not be entered before December 31 of that year. If you do not want to file a joint return, a divorce on or before December 31 would likely be best.

13.10 What tax consequences should I consider regarding the sale of our home?

When your home is sold, whether during your divorce or after, the sale may be subject to a *capital gains tax.* If your home was your primary residence and you lived in the home for two of the preceding five years, you may be eligible to exclude up to $250,000 of the capital gain on the sale of your home. If both you and your spouse meet the ownership and residence tests, you may be eligible to exclude up to $500,000 of the gain.

If you anticipate the gain on the sale of your residence to be over $250,000, talk with your attorney early in the divorce process about a plan to minimize the tax liability. For more information, see *IRS Publication 523, Selling Your Home,* or visit the IRS website at www.irs.gov, and talk with your tax advisor.

13.11 How might capital gains tax be a problem for me years after the divorce?

Future capital gains tax on the sale of property should be discussed with your attorney during the negotiation and trial preparation stages of your case. This is especially important if the sale of the property is imminent. Failure to do so may result in an unfair outcome. For example, suppose you agree that your spouse will be awarded the proceeds from the sale of your home expected to net $200,000 after the real estate commission, and you will take the stock portfolio also valued at $200,000.

Suppose that after the divorce, you decide to sell the stock. It is still valued at $200,000, but you learn that its original price was $120,000 and that you must pay capital gains tax of 15 percent on the $80,000 of gain. You pay tax of $12,000, leaving you with $188,000.

Meanwhile, your former spouse sells the marital home but pays no capital gains tax because he qualifies for the $250,000 exemption. He is left with the full $200,000. Tax implications of your property division should always be discussed with your attorney, with support from your tax advisor as needed.

13.12 During and after the divorce, who gets to claim the child as a dependent?

Under federal law, the parent who has custody of the child for more than one half of the year may claim the child as a dependent on his or her income tax return. However, the judge has authority, or the parties may agree, to allocate the dependency exemptions between the parties. If a dependency exemption is allocated to the noncustodial parent, the custodial parent will have to sign *IRS Form 8332.*

13.13 Do I have to pay taxes on the portion of my spouse's 401(k) that was awarded to me in the divorce?

No. If the transfer of retirement benefits is from your spouse's retirement account directly to a retirement account in your name (usually an IRA), there are no taxes due from either party.

13.14 Is the cost of getting a divorce, including my attorney fees, tax deductible under any circumstances?

Your legal fees for getting a divorce are not deductible. However, a portion of your attorney fees may be deductible if they are for:

•The collection of sums included in your gross income, such as alimony or interest income

•Advice regarding the determination of taxes or tax due

Attorney fees are "miscellaneous" deductions for individuals and are consequently limited to 2 percent of your adjusted gross income. More details can be found in *IRS Publication 529, Miscellaneous Deductions.*

You may also be able to deduct fees you pay to appraisers or accountants who help. Talk to your tax advisor about whether any portion of your attorney fees or other expenses from your divorce are deductible.

13.15 Do I have to complete a new Form W-4 for my employer because of my divorce?

Completing a new *Form W-4, Employee's Withholding Certificate,* will help you to claim the proper withholding allowances based upon your marital status and exemptions. If you are receiving spousal support, you may need to make quarterly estimated tax payments. Consult with your tax advisor to obtain tax planning advice.

13.16 What is *innocent spouse relief* and how can it help me?

Innocent spouse relief refers to a method of obtaining relief from the Internal Revenue Service for taxes owed as a result of a joint income tax return filed during your marriage. Numerous factors affect your eligibility for innocent spouse tax relief. See *IRS Publication 971, Innocent Spouse Relief,* for more information.

Talk with your attorney or your tax advisor if you are concerned about liability for taxes arising from joint tax returns filed during the marriage. You may benefit from a referral to an attorney who specializes in tax law.

14

Name Change

Many women change their names when they marry. Once it is clear that a divorce is inevitable, it is not unusual for a woman to wish to return to her maiden name. (Most divorce issues apply equally to men and women. This is an exception as it is much less common for men to change their names when marrying, though there are men who have changed their names to a hyphenated name. The answers provided below apply equally to men and women.)

14.1   Can I change my name when I get divorced?

Yes, you can change your name as part of the divorce, or by a separate petition filed with the circuit court where you reside.

14.2   Can I change my name before the divorce is filed?

Yes, you can seek a name change at any time, independently of a divorce action.

14.3   Is there any time limit regarding when I change my name? Can I change my name after the divorce is over?

There is no time limit regarding when you are able to change your name. You can seek a name change before your divorce, during your divorce, or at any time after your divorce.

14.4 What's the procedure for changing my name?

You file a petition to change your name in the circuit court in the city or county where you reside. The form *Application for Change of Name (Adult)* is available on Virginia's Judicial System website at www.courts.state.va.us/forms/circuit/cc1411.pdf. You have to complete the form and sign it under oath before a notary public. You then submit the signed application, the required filing fee, and a name-change order to the circuit court. The court will review your application and more than likely enter an order changing your name without a hearing. Your attorney can assist you with this paperwork.

14.5 Can my spouse oppose my name change?

No, if you file a separate petition for your name change, your spouse (or ex-spouse) is not even notified.

14.6 If I change my name, do I have to return to my maiden name?

No, you can return to your maiden name, return to a prior married name, or change to a new name. The restrictions are that your name change cannot be for a fraudulent purpose and cannot infringe upon the rights of others.

14.7 I have custody of my child. Can I change his name to match my new married name?

It depends. If the child's father agrees and joins in the application, then a judge will likely approve the name change without a hearing. If the father does not join in the application, then the court will provide notice to the father and allow him an opportunity to object. If the father objects, then the judge will have a hearing to determine whether the name change is in the best interest of the child. A judge will usually not allow a name change over the objection of the father if the father is a fairly normal father. The judge will generally only order a name change over the objection of the father if:

- The father has abandoned the child.
- The father has engaged in sufficient misconduct to embarrass the child in continued use of the father's name.

- The child otherwise will be harmed by continuing to bear the father's name.
- The child desires that his name be changed and is of sufficient age and discretion to make such a choice.

14.8 What's the procedure if I want to try to change my child's name?

You apply to change your child's name in the circuit court in the city or county where the child resides. The form *Application for Change of Name (Minor)* is available on Virginia's Judicial System website at www.courts.state.va.us/forms/circuit/cc1427.pdf. You will complete the application and sign it under oath before a notary public. If the child's father is joining in the application, you will have him sign the application under oath before a notary public. You will then submit the signed application, required filing fee, and a proposed name-change order to the circuit court. A hearing will be necessary if the other parent does not agree. Your attorney can assist with this paperwork and with the hearing, if necessary.

15

Settlement Issues,
Options, and Strategy

It is a rare person who doesn't want to settle his or her divorce issues. In almost every divorce case, both parties have a strong preference for settlement versus a trial with the judge deciding the issues. The problem is that each party wants to settle on terms that are acceptable to him or her, and those terms are often unacceptable to the other party. The settlement process involves communications and compromises to bridge those differences and arrive at an agreed-upon result in which both parties are somewhat unhappy with the outcome.

What is the best way to settle a divorce case? There is no one-size-fits-all settlement procedure that is the best for everyone. Instead, it is important to know and understand the options, and to select the option that is most likely to work for you and your spouse.

What issues can be resolved by agreement? Does an agreement have to be in writing? How does timing factor into the settlement process? What is the best settlement strategy to follow? This chapter deals with these and related questions.

15.1 What is the most simple, least expensive option for settling a divorce case?

You and your spouse can sit down at the kitchen table, make a list of the issues, discuss options and compromises, and try to reach an agreement on all issues. If you choose this most basic approach, you should each obtain legal advice first. If you obtain legal advice after reaching a tentative agreement, and then change your position on issues based on that advice,

116

that will almost certainly anger the other side and may make settlement more difficult than if you had obtained legal advice first. It is a common mistake to begin discussions before obtaining legal advice and preparing for negotiations.

15.2   What advice should I follow before beginning negotiations with my spouse?

Make sure you understand the facts (such as financial details) and the applicable law before you begin to negotiate. Mistakes, sometimes serious, are made in divorce cases by people who begin negotiating in ignorance of the relevant facts and the applicable law. Sometimes these serious mistakes cannot be undone. Do your due diligence first. This is important.

15.3   Should I negotiate directly with my spouse?

If you understand the finances and any other facts, if you have obtained legal advice and understand what would happen if you went to court, and if you are the dominant party (the spouse most likely to get his or her way in an argument or dispute with the other spouse), then it probably is in your interests to negotiate directly. If your spouse is dominant and you are concerned that he or she may pressure you into an agreement that is not in your best interests, then you should not negotiate directly with your spouse. Instead, you need an advocate to negotiate on your behalf.

15.4   My spouse and I want to negotiate directly with each other without attorneys, but we have problems communicating. What are our options?

Your best option may be to hire a mediator. You should hire either a respected divorce attorney or a retired judge who has handled divorce cases. (A non-attorney mediator may be adequate for single issues such as the visitation schedule.) A *mediator* is neutral and does not act as an advocate for either party. If both parties agree, an attorney or retired judge mediator can explain the applicable law. This explanation occurs in communications with both parties.

The mediator is not an advocate, nor is he or she a decision-maker. The mediator does not function as a judge deciding issues upon which you and spouse cannot agree. Instead, the

117

mediator is a facilitator. The mediator makes efforts to ensure that the communications between you and your spouse are civil and constructive, that you both hear and understand the other's perspective, and that different options to resolve the disputes are considered.

If you are able to settle issues with the help of the mediator, he or she can draft a written settlement agreement. You and your spouse will be encouraged to review the agreement with your own attorneys before signing.

15.5 My spouse and I want to negotiate with each other, but we want our attorneys involved. What are our options?

You, your spouse, and the two attorneys could meet for *negotiation* (such a meeting is sometimes referred to as a *settlement conference);* the four of you could meet with a mediator; or you and your spouse could each hire a collaborative attorney and pursue a collaborative divorce.

15.6 What is *collaborative divorce*?

Collaborative divorce is a process in which each party hires his or her own collaboratively trained attorney. The attorneys and the parties have a series of meetings (attended by both parties and their attorneys), during which they discuss the parties' situation, identify values, discuss issues, explore options, and seek agreement.

At the beginning of the process, the parties and the attorneys sign a contract agreeing that neither attorney will file nor be involved in the divorce court case. Consequently, if the collaborative process does not result in a settlement, the parties need to hire new divorce lawyers to proceed.

15.7 Should I suggest to my spouse that we use the collaborative divorce process?

The collaborative divorce process is a good fit for some divorcing couples. To determine if it is a good fit for you, ask yourself the following questions:

First: Are you and your spouse able to sit in the same room and discuss your issues constructively? This is a basic requirement of the collaborative process.

118

Second: Do you trust your spouse to make full disclosure of all information relevant to the divorce negotiations, even those facts helpful to you? The collaborative process is based upon and requires full disclosure by both spouses.

Third: Are you and your spouse likely to both be willing to make the difficult concessions that will be required to reach a settlement without the pressure of an upcoming trial? In most divorce cases, settlement occurs only when both parties make compromises that they do not want to make. In non-collaborative cases, settlement often occurs in response to an upcoming hearing or trial that forces both parties to consider what would happen in the absence of a settlement. In the collaborative process, the attorneys are prohibited from using the litigation process as a pressure to obtain a settlement.

15.8　My spouse and I cannot communicate directly in a constructive manner, and I do not want to meet with him. What settlement options do I have?

This is probably the most common divorce situation. (Let's face it, if you and your spouse were great at communicating constructively with each other and successfully resolving your differences, you probably wouldn't be getting divorced.) In this standard model, the attorneys share information, informally or through the discovery process. One side or the other then prepares a proposed settlement agreement, reviews and discusses it with his or her client, makes whatever edits are needed, and then sends the proposed agreement to the other attorney. The other attorney reviews and discusses it with his or her client, and either accepts the offer, or (more likely) makes a counterproposal. As long as each party responds each time with a concession or compromise, this process will eventually result in a settlement.

This is a flexible process. If the parties wish, they can meet to discuss any issue at any time, they can meet with each other with the attorneys present, or a mediator can be brought in to assist in the settlement process.

15.9 My spouse and I are in agreement regarding most of our divorce issues. Does our agreement have to be in writing?

Yes, your agreement has to be in writing. Oral agreements between husband and wife are not enforceable.

15.10 My spouse and I have been negotiating for eight months and aren't making any progress. What should I do?

You should talk with your attorney about alternative procedures for reaching a settlement. You should consider whether the passing of time may resolve issues or otherwise make settlement more likely. If so, consider taking a break from negotiations. You should consider whether it makes sense to pursue a limited settlement on the issues on which you agree, if you cannot reach a settlement on all issues. Finally, if you reach the point at which you want things resolved, and you cannot agree, then instruct your attorney to arrange to have the issue or issues resolved by the judge. Realize that it may take months, or even more than a year in some jurisdictions, to get into court for a hearing or trial, so make your plans taking that delay into account.

15.11 If I decide to file for divorce and have a trial scheduled, can I can continue to try to settle?

Yes. Scheduling a case for hearing or a trial is often helpful in reaching a settlement, as it forces both parties to seriously consider what would happen in the absence of a settlement, and it creates a deadline. This often results in both parties being willing to make compromises in order to settle to avoid trial.

15.12 If my spouse and I are able to settle, do we still have to go to court?

No. One of you will still have to file for divorce (if you haven't already), but your attorneys will be able to submit the necessary paperwork by mail so that you and your spouse will not have to appear in court.

15.13 Is mediation mandatory?

In some courts you are required to attend at least an introductory mediation session.

15.14 If my spouse and I are unable to settle, will the judge learn about what happened in mediation?

No, mediation (and other settlement negotiations as a general rule, with exceptions) is confidential.

15.15 What types of issues can be mediated or negotiated?

Nearly all divorce issues can be resolved by agreement.

15.16 How do I prepare for mediation or for a settlement conference?

You should have a good understanding of the finances and any other factual details relevant to the issues to be resolved. You should understand the applicable Virginia law, and what would happen if the case does not settle and goes to court.

You should have your attorney prepare a written settlement proposal representing your opening negotiating position. You should consider ways in which you could compromise in order to reach a settlement. You should consider what is important to your spouse, and ways in which a compromise could meet the concerns of both parties.

Spend time analyzing both sides' interests and positions. Read and think about negotiating. Recognize that your spouse is no longer your trusted ally. It is often difficult for at least one of the parties (usually the one that does not want the divorce) to make the mental transition necessary to recognize that divorce negotiations are very different from the normal discussions that occurred during the marriage when the parties were still partners.

It is dangerous to rely upon your instincts for negotiations. It is better to rely upon your knowledge of the issues to be discussed, your preparations, and your attorney. Recognize that your spouse is almost certainly not looking to you for advice. In fact, he or she probably interprets your advice as self-serving and is primarily interested in what you say because of the clues it provides regarding your positions and intentions.

Many spouses recoil at the idea that he or she is in a negotiation in which what he says, or how he says it, can be detrimental to the outcome that he seeks. There are probably numerous ways in which your divorce is not to your liking, including this. Whether you like it or not, there are probably a number of issues in your divorce that are going to be resolved by agreement, so it makes sense for you to be as effective as possible as a negotiator. Even if your attorney is handling the negotiations, it is important that you understand the settlement issues and dynamics so that you can further, rather than inadvertently undercut, your positions.

15.17 I want my attorney to look over the agreements my spouse and I discussed in mediation before I give my final approval. Is this possible?

Yes, you should not sign any agreement without legal advice.

15.18 Who pays for mediation?

That is typically an item to be negotiated. Many parties pay for the mediation with marital funds.

15.19 What happens if my spouse and I settle some, but not all, of the issues in our divorce?

Any issues that you and your spouse cannot resolve by agreement can be decided by the judge.

15.20 After our divorce is final, can the settlement agreement be modified by a judge?

Your agreement regarding the division of assets and debts and spousal support cannot be modified without both parties' consent. Child custody, visitation, and child support can be modified by the judge if there is a material change in circumstances.

15.21 Can my spouse and I modify our settlement agreement after the divorce is final?

Yes, though to be enforceable your new agreement will have to be in writing, and may have to be part of a new court order.

15.22 What is a *property settlement agreement*?

There are a number of different names for a *divorce settlement agreement,* including *divorce and property settlement agreement.* Regardless of the title, the agreement typically provides that the divorce will be on no-fault grounds, identifies and allocates the assets and debts, addresses spousal support, provides details regarding the custody and visitation arrangements, sets child support, and deals with other issues that need to be covered.

15.23 What happens after my spouse and I approve the property settlement agreement? Do we still have to go to court?

If your agreement with your spouse resolves all of the issues, then you will probably not go to court. Instead, the attorneys will submit the final divorce paperwork to the court by mail.

15.24 If my spouse and I think our settlement agreement is fair, why does the judge have to approve it?

The judge does not have to approve your agreement regarding property division and spousal support. The judge will review your agreement regarding custody, visitation, and child support to ensure the best interests of your children are being met. In practice, judges nearly always approve divorce agreements.

15.25 My divorce is scheduled for trial. Does this mean there is no hope for a settlement?

Many cases are settled after a trial date is set. The setting of a trial date may cause you and your spouse to think about the risks and costs of going to trial. This can help you and your spouse focus on what is most important to you, and lead to a negotiated settlement. Because the costs of preparing for and proceeding to trial are substantial, it is best to engage in settlement negotiations well in advance of your trial date. However, it is not uncommon for cases to settle shortly before trial.

16

Documents Filed in Court

Marriage is a legal status regulated by the state. To end a marriage one of the parties has to file a lawsuit seeking a divorce. This chapter addresses questions regarding the documents filed in a divorce lawsuit. Lawyers refer to these documents as *pleadings*.

16.1   What is a *complaint for divorce*?
A *complaint for divorce* is the first pleading or court paper filed with a circuit court that initiates the divorce case.

16.2   What is contained in a complaint?
A complaint contains allegations and a request for relief. The allegations include the parties' names, the date and place of the marriage, information regarding any children, information regarding the separation, and other required information.

The request for relief identifies for the judge and the other party what you are seeking in the divorce case. Requested relief includes a divorce, and may include in addition a request for the following:

- the assets and debts be divided (equitable distribution)
- spousal support be awarded
- custody and visitation be determined
- child support be set, and that attorney's fees be awarded

This is a typical, but not exclusive, list.

16.3   Do I have to file a complaint?

Either you or your spouse has to file a complaint for divorce if you want to get divorced. There is no alternative.

16.4   I am anxious to get divorced. How soon can I file a complaint?

You may file as soon as you have an available ground for divorce. (*See* chapter 7 for details regarding the grounds of divorce.)

16.5   I came home from work and there was a complaint and other paperwork in a plastic bag hanging on my doorknob. What do I have to do?

You have been served with the initial divorce paperwork. You should immediately hire an attorney as you are required to file your answer within twenty-one days.

16.6   I want to file a complaint, but I do not want the sheriff delivering the paperwork to my spouse while she has the children. What are my options?

Your attorney can help you explore the options, which include having your spouse sign an acceptance of service form, having her attorney voluntarily file an answer, or having your spouse served while the children are with you.

16.7   What is an *answer* and when does it have to be filed?

An *answer* is your written response to your spouse's complaint. Your answer has to be filed in the clerk's office of the circuit court within twenty-one days of the service of the complaint on you.

16.8   What is a *counterclaim* and is it required?

If your spouse files a complaint, then you will have to file an answer. If you also wish to request relief from the judge (including a divorce, equitable distribution, spousal support, custody and visitation, child support, and attorney's fees), then you should file a *counterclaim* in addition to your answer. A counterclaim also protects you against a nonsuit. Discuss this with your attorney.

16.9   What are *motions?*

A *motion* is a written request filed in your divorce case. There are many types of issues that can develop during a divorce case. For example, these issues may arise during the case but before trial:

- Who gets possession of the house?
- What is the visitation schedule?
- How much support should be paid?
- Who is responsible for what bills?

Disputes sometimes arise during discovery that result in motions being filed. There are many different motions that may be filed, including motions for attorney's fees, motions to compel, and motions for divorce. Either side can file motions, which are requests to the judge to make rulings resolving specific issues in dispute. Motions are typically, but not always, considered and ruled on by the judge prior to trial.

16.10   What are *petitions?*

A *petition* is a request for relief filed with the court, similar to a complaint or a motion.

16.11   What are *orders?*

An *order* is a document signed by the judge reflecting one or more rulings made by the judge. The parties are legally obligated to comply with all orders entered in their case.

16.12   What are the most common orders in a divorce case?

The most common order in a divorce case is a *divorce order* (an order granting divorce). The divorce order may address all of the issues, including equitable distribution, spousal support, custody and visitation, child support, and attorney's fees. Alternatively, some of these issues can be addressed in separate orders. There is usually an order entered for each hearing and following the trial, if there is a trial. If you settle all of your issues, the settlement agreement is usually incorporated in the divorce order (your agreement becomes part of the order).

Other common orders include *scheduling orders* (setting dates and deadlines for your preparations for trial), and *pendente lite orders* which govern temporary issues such as possession of the home, custody, visitation, and support until trial.

16.13 Is a divorce order necessary even if we have a settlement agreement?

Yes, the divorce occurs when the divorce order is signed by the judge.

17

Discovery

The *Rules of the Supreme Court of Virginia* provides for the process of *discovery* for parties in a lawsuit (including a divorce case) to gain information from each other and from third parties pertaining to the issues in the lawsuit. This chapter will answer your questions regarding interrogatories, requests for production of documents, requests for admission, depositions, and subpoenas *duces tecum*. Please note that these discovery options are only available once a complaint has been filed instituting a divorce case in the court.

17.1   What are *interrogatories*?

Interrogatories are written questions that each party is allowed to send to the other party. For example, if you don't know how much your spouse earns, your attorney can send him an interrogatory requesting that information. Interrogatories are written by the attorneys and typically sent in a set of one or two dozen questions. The party receiving the interrogatories is required to provide, within twenty-one days, written answers under oath. (*Under oath* means that the party providing the answers must appear before a notary and swear or affirm that the answers are true.)

17.2   What are *requests for production of documents*?

In most cases each side has documents that the other side needs to review to analyze settlement and to prepare for trial. Each party is allowed to send to the other side written *requests for documents* relevant to the issues in the case. The party receiving the requests is required to respond within twenty-one days, and to produce those documents in his or her possession or control.

17.3   What are *requests for admission?*

Either attorney may send *requests for admission* to the other party requiring him or her to admit or deny certain statements relevant to the case. For example, your attorney may send a request to the other party asking him or her to admit the value of marital assets. This is often a good way to narrow issues for trial. For example, if the other party admits the value of the marital home (agrees with you) then an appraisal is not necessary and that issue is resolved. Requests for admission are in writing, and the other party has to respond in writing within twenty-one days.

17.4   What are *depositions?*

A *deposition* is a means of discovery in which the parties and their counsel meet at the office of one of the attorneys, with a court reporter present, and the attorneys question the person being deposed while the court reporter records the questions and the answers. The person being deposed has to swear or affirm at the beginning of the process that he or she will tell the truth. It is not unusual for both parties, and sometimes others, to be deposed on the same day.

17.5   What are *subpoenas duces tecum?*

A *subpoena duces tecum* is a document prepared by one of the attorneys that is sent to a person or a company requiring the production of documents relevant to the case. This discovery device is similar to a request for production of documents, but a request for production is sent to a party to the case, and a subpoena *duces tecum* is sent to a nonparty. For example, your attorney may decide to send a subpoena *duces tecum* to your spouse's employer to obtain his employment contract, benefit information, and specific work schedule.

17.6   How long does the discovery process take?

This varies from case to case as there is no fixed duration provided by the *Rules of the Supreme Court of Virginia*. Once a trial is scheduled, it is common for a scheduling order to be entered by the judge providing time limits for the completion of discovery.

17.7   My lawyer insists that we conduct discovery, but I don't want to spend the time and money on it. Is it really necessary?

In most divorce cases each side needs information from the other in order to analyze settlement options and to prepare for trial. Your concern is legitimate as discovery can be very expensive. It is important to work with your attorney throughout your divorce case to make sure that appropriate cost/benefit decisions are being made. For example, if there is $100,000 or custody in dispute, it makes sense to be willing to spend more time and money than if only $5,000 or a minor visitation issue were in dispute. It is important that your attorney tailor his or her approach to the specific issues and disputes in your case, and your preferences.

17.8   Is there a way to gain the information my attorney needs without the expense of discovery?

You can help control the expense of discovery by providing as much information as possible to your attorney. The more complete and better organized the documentation you provide is, the less time your attorney will have to spend. In addition, you and your spouse can cooperate in freely sharing information between you, which should also reduce attorney's fees.

17.9   I just received from my spouse's attorney interrogatories and requests that I produce documents. My lawyer wants me to respond within twenty-one days. I'll never make the deadline. What I can do?

You need to make a good-faith effort to provide what you can within the deadline. Your attorney should still respond within the twenty-one day deadline providing all available information, and stating any objections that he or she may have.

The initial responses can then be supplemented once you are able to complete your work.

17.10 I don't have access to my documents, and my spouse is being uncooperative in providing my lawyer with information. Can my lawyer request information directly from an employer or financial institution?

Yes, using a subpoena *duces tecum* which requires the person or corporation to produce the documentation.

17.11 My spouse's lawyer intends to subpoena my medical records. Aren't those private?

Your medical records may be relevant to issues in the case, including custody and visitation, equitable distribution, and spousal support. If your physical or mental condition is at issue in your case, then the opposing counsel will be able to obtain relevant records.

17.12 My spouse's attorney has sent me interrogatories and requests for production of documents for information that is not relevant to our divorce case. Do I have to respond?

Your attorney will review every discovery request from the other party, and will make objection to any interrogatory or request that he or she feels is improper based upon Virginia law.

17.13 My spouse's attorney objected to many interrogatories that my attorney believes are legitimate and proper. Is there any way we can force my spouse to answer?

Yes, your attorney will first send a letter to the other attorney requesting complete responses. If the other attorney persists with his objections, your attorney can file a motion to compel and obtain a hearing at which she will ask the judge to order your spouse to respond.

17.14 I own my business. Will I have to disclose my business records?

If your business records are relevant to your case—which they almost certainly are if your case involves equitable distribution, spousal support, or child support—then you will have to produce those records.

17.15 It's been two months since my lawyer sent interrogatories to my spouse, and we still don't have his answers. I answered mine on time. Is there anything that can be done to speed up the process?

Yes, your attorney may file a motion to compel and obtain a hearing to ask the judge to order the other side to respond. Your attorney should send a letter to the opposing counsel requesting responses before he files the motion to compel.

17.16 What is the purpose of a *deposition?*

The purpose of a *deposition* is to gain information helpful to your case and harmful to your spouse's case. The specific purposes of a deposition vary from case to case and witness to witness. Your attorney may be seeking answers to questions and specific admissions.

17.17 Will what I say in my deposition be used against me when we go to court?

Possibly. The transcript of your deposition can be admitted into evidence at trial, so the judge will become aware of your deposition testimony if your deposition transcript is admitted into evidence.

17.18 How should I prepare for my deposition?

You should talk to your attorney about the exact procedure so that you fully understand the process in advance. You should receive advice from your attorney about what approach you should use. You are under oath and you must tell the truth, but with many questions you have the option of providing short, limited answers, or longer, more detailed and explanatory answers. You should be polite and avoid sarcasm. You don't want the judge to read rude or sarcastic answers, as you want the judge to have a favorable impression of you.

Finally, the more fully you understand your case, the exact issues, the facts, and the applicable law, the better prepared you will be. Be truthful as your integrity is paramount. You want the judge to trust and believe your testimony.

17.19 What will I be asked at my deposition?

Your attorney will help you prepare based upon the exact issues in the case. If your case involves custody and visitation, equitable distribution, or spousal support, you should be familiar with the statutory factors relevant to those issues.

17.20 Can I refuse to answer questions at my deposition?

The general rule is that you have to answer the questions. However, your attorney can object if any of the questions are improper. And you can refuse to answer based upon the Fifth Amendment to the United States Constitution if your answer would implicate you in a crime. The Fifth Amendment comes up most frequently in divorce cases regarding adultery. If adultery is an issue in your case, be sure to discuss this with your attorney in advance of your deposition.

17.21 What if I give incorrect information in my deposition?

You are under oath so you should not intentionally give incorrect information. If you later learn that you inadvertently gave incorrect information, let your attorney know so that she can advise opposing counsel and correct the record.

17.22 What if I don't know or can't remember the answer to a question?

Then that is your answer. You are not required to guess or speculate.

17.23 Are depositions always necessary?

No, depositions are optional. A deposition should be taken when that is the best way to gain the information your attorney seeks, or if it's important to determine exactly how a party or other witness would testify.

17.24 Does every witness have to be deposed?

No, your attorney should depose only those opposing witnesses who are important enough to justify the expense associated with a deposition. A deposition is probably not necessary if the witness is willing to be interviewed by your attorney.

17.25 Will I get a copy of the depositions in my case?

That depends upon whether transcripts are ordered. The court reporter charges a fee for coming to the depositions and making a record of the questions and answers. The court reporter charges an additional fee for creating a transcript by typing the questions and answers. You will receive a copy of the depositions only if your attorney orders and you pay for the transcripts.

18

Hearings and Trial

For many of us, our images of going to court are based upon movie scenes and television shows. We picture the witness breaking down in tears after a grueling cross-examination. We see lawyers moving around the courtroom, waving their arms as they argue their case to the jury.

The reality, however, is usually quite different. Going to court for your divorce can mean many things, ranging from sitting in a hallway waiting for your case to be called, to being on the witness stand giving answers to mundane questions about your monthly living expenses.

Regardless of the nature of your court proceeding, going to court often evokes a sense of anxiety. Your divorce might be the first time in your life you have been in a courtroom. Be assured that your feelings of nervousness and uncertainty are normal.

Understanding what will occur in court, and being well prepared for any court hearings will relieve much of your stress. Knowing the order of events, the role of the people in the courtroom, etiquette in the courtroom, and what is expected of you will make the entire experience easier.

18.1   What do I need to know about appearing in court and court dates in general?

Court dates are important. As soon as you receive a notice from your attorney about a court date in your case, confirm whether your attendance will be required and put it on your calendar.

Ask your attorney about the nature of the hearing, including whether the judge will be listening to testimony by witnesses, or merely listening to the arguments of the lawyers.

Ask whether it is necessary for you to meet with your attorney or take any other action to prepare for the hearing, such as providing additional information or documents.

Find out how long the hearing is expected to last. It may be as short as a few minutes or as long as a day or more.

If you plan to attend the hearing, determine where and when to meet your attorney. Depending upon the type of hearing, your lawyer may want you to arrive in advance of the scheduled hearing time to prepare.

Make sure you know the location of the courthouse, where to park, and the floor and room number of the courtroom. Planning for such simple matters as having change available for a parking meter can eliminate unnecessary stress. If you want someone to go to court with you to provide you support, check with your attorney first.

18.2   When and how often will I need to go to court?

Whether and how often you will need to go to court depends upon a number of factors. Depending upon the complexity of your case, you may have only one hearing or numerous court hearings throughout the course of your divorce.

Some hearings, usually those on procedural matters, are typically attended only by the attorneys (though clients may attend all hearings). These could include requests for the other side to provide information, or for the setting of certain deadlines. Other hearings, such as temporary hearings for custody or support, are typically attended by both parties and their attorneys.

If you and your spouse settle all of the issues in your case, although not required, you can choose to testify at a final hearing in which the judge will review and sign your divorce order.

If your case proceeds to trial, your appearance will be required for the duration of the trial.

18.3   Will there be a jury at my divorce trial?

No, divorce cases are handled by a judge without a jury.

18.4   How much notice will I receive about appearing in court?

The amount of notice you will receive for any court hearing can vary from a few days to several weeks. A trial is typically scheduled for months and even a year in advance. Ask your attorney whether and when it will be necessary for you to appear in court on your case so that you can plan and prepare as needed.

If you receive notice of a hearing, contact your attorney immediately. He can tell you whether your appearance is required, and what other preparations are needed.

18.5   Once my complaint for divorce is filed, how soon can a temporary hearing be held to decide what happens with our child and our finances while the divorce is pending?

How quickly a temporary or *pendente lite* hearing can be held varies among jurisdictions. This is an issue to consider and discuss with your attorney in analyzing in which court to file.

18.6   I am afraid to be alone in the same room with my spouse. When I go to court, is this going to happen if the lawyers go into the judge's office to discuss the case?

Prior to any court hearing or trial, you and your spouse may be asked to wait while your attorneys meet with the judge to discuss preliminary matters. A number of options are likely to be available to ensure that you feel safe. These might include having you or your spouse wait in different locations or having a friend or family member present. The bailiff (a deputy sheriff) is nearly always present in the courtroom. In addition, a deputy clerk and a court reporter are sometimes present.

Your lawyer wants to support you in feeling secure throughout all court proceedings. Just let you attorney know your concerns.

18.7 Do I have to go to court every time there is a court hearing on any motion?

It's your case, so the best practice is to plan to attend all hearings. That being said, there are some hearings (such as a scheduling hearing) at which your appearance would provide little or no benefit to you or your case. Talk to your attorney before each hearing to discuss the issues to be addressed at the hearing, and whether your attendance is required or would be of benefit to you or your case.

18.8 My spouse's lawyer keeps asking for *continuances* of court dates. Is there anything I can do to stop this?

A *continuance* is a delay or postponement of a court hearing or trial. Your attorney can oppose any request for a continuance. Judges typically require a sufficient reason before a court date is continued.

18.9 If I have to go to court, will I be put on the stand to testify?

You are likely to have to testify at any court appearance, including trial, at which evidence is submitted. Some hearings involve only legal arguments so you would not have to testify in that situation. Talk to your attorney in advance of any court appearance to find out whether you will need to testify.

18.10 My lawyer said I need to be in court for our *temporary hearing* next week. What's going to happen?

A *temporary hearing,* often referred to as a *pendente lite* hearing, may be held to determine preliminary issues such as who remains in the house while your divorce is pending, temporary custody and visitation, temporary support, and other preliminary financial matters. *Pendente lite* means pending the litigation, and the temporary ruling typically lasts until the final divorce rulings have been made.

The procedure for your temporary hearing can vary depending upon the county or city in which your case was filed, and the judge to which the case is assigned. In some jurisdictions your hearing will be one of numerous other hearings on the judge's calendar. You may find yourself in a courtroom with other lawyers and their clients, all having matters scheduled before the judge that day.

You and other witnesses may be required to take the witness stand to give testimony at your temporary hearing. If this is the case, meeting with your attorney in advance to fully prepare is very important. Talk to your lawyer in advance about the procedure you should expect for the temporary hearing in your case.

18.11 Do I have to go to court if all of the issues in my case are settled?

No, as a general rule. The exception is when the case is settled immediately before trial and there is not adequate time to prepare a written settlement agreement to be signed. In that situation, the parties and counsel would appear in court, the agreement would be stated aloud in the presence of the judge and the court reporter, and the parties affirm the agreement on the record. The divorce evidence could then be presented at the same time. Typically when a case is settled in advance of trial, the necessary evidence and paperwork is submitted to the clerk's office by mail or delivery, and neither party appears in court before the judge.

18.12 Are there any rules about courtroom etiquette that I need to know?

Following are a few tips:

- Dress appropriately. Avoid overly casual dress, excessive jewelry, revealing clothing, and extreme hairstyles.

- Don't bring beverages into the courtroom. Most courts have rules that do not allow food and drink in courtrooms. If you need water, ask your lawyer.

- Dispose of chewing gum before giving testimony.

- Don't talk aloud in the courtroom unless you're on the witness stand or being questioned by the judge.

- Stand up whenever the judge is entering or leaving the courtroom.

- Most courts do not allow parties to bring electronic devices into the courtroom. Check with your attorney in advance. If you have an electronic device in court, make sure it is turned off.
- Be mindful that the judge may be observing you and those you bring to the hearing, so maintain an appropriate demeanor at all times.

18.13 What is the role of the *bailiff?*

The *bailiff* is a deputy sheriff who is responsible for courtroom security.

18.14 Will there be a *court reporter,* and what will he or she do?

A *court reporter* is a professional trained to make an accurate record of the words spoken and documents offered into evidence during court proceedings. A written transcript of a court proceeding may be purchased from the court reporter. If your case is appealed, the transcript prepared by the court reporter will be used by the appeals court to review the details of your trial.

A court reporter will be present in court for your case only if requested by one of the attorneys. You should have a court reporter present for all important hearings and the trial. Without a court reporter there is no accurate record of the proceedings for purpose of an appeal.

18.15 Will I be able to talk to my attorney while we are in court?

During court proceedings it is important that your attorney give his undivided attention to anything being said by the judge, witnesses, or your spouse's lawyer. For this reason, your attorney will avoid talking with you when anyone else in the courtroom is speaking.

It is critical that your attorney hear each question asked by the other lawyer and all answers given by each witness. If not, opportunities for making objections to inappropriate evidence may be lost. You can support your attorney in doing an effective job for you by avoiding talking to him while a court hearing is in progress.

Plan to have pen and paper with you when you go to court. If your court proceeding is underway and your lawyer is listening to what is being said by others in the courtroom, write him a note with your questions or comments.

If your court hearing is lengthy, breaks will be taken. You can use this time to discuss with your attorney any questions or observations you have about the proceeding.

18.16 What questions might my lawyer ask me about the problems in our marriage, and why I want the divorce?

That depends upon the issues in the case. In some cases there is little focus on why the marriage failed. In other cases, one or both parties attempt to show that the other party is to blame and is at fault for the divorce. It is common to focus on fault if equitable distribution or spousal support are at issue in the case.

18.17 My lawyer said that the judge has issued a *pretrial order* having to do with my upcoming trial and that we'll have to "comply" with it. What does this mean?

Pretrial scheduling orders are common in divorce cases. These orders establish deadlines that have to be met leading up to trial. Though the exact terms of these orders vary, they commonly establish deadlines for completing discovery, for identifying expert witnesses, and for disclosing witnesses and trial exhibits. You and your attorney should plan and prepare in order to meet or comply with the terms of the pretrial order.

18.18 What is a *pretrial conference?*

A *pretrial conference* is a meeting attended by the lawyers, the parties, and the judge to review information related to an upcoming trial, such as:

- how long the trial is expected to last
- the issues in dispute
- the law surrounding the disputed issues
- the identification of witnesses
- trial exhibits
- the status of negotiations

Pretrial conferences are scheduled in some, but not all, cases.

18.19 Besides meeting with my lawyer, is there anything else I should do to prepare for my upcoming trial?

Yes, be sure to review your deposition and any information you provided in your discovery, such as answers to interrogatories. Also be sure to review any exhibits that will be introduced at trial. At trial, it is possible that you will be asked some of the same questions you answered in your deposition or at a prior hearing. If you think you might give different answers at trial, discuss this with your lawyer in advance. It is important that your attorney know in advance of trial whether any information you provided during the discovery process has changed.

18.20 I'm meeting with my lawyer to prepare for trial. How do I make the most of these meetings?

Meeting with your lawyer to prepare for your trial is important to achieving a good outcome. Come to the meeting prepared to discuss the following:

- the issues in your case
- your desired outcome on each of the issues
- the questions you might be asked at trial by both lawyers
- the exhibits that will be offered into evidence during the trial
- the witnesses for your trial
- the status of negotiations

Your meeting with your lawyer will help you better understand what to expect at your trial, and will help your attorney prepare to do her best on your behalf.

**18.21 My lawyer says that the law firm is busy with _trial prep-_
aration. What exactly is my lawyer doing to prepare
for my trial?**

Countless tasks are necessary to prepare your case for
trial. Following are several of the most common:

- Developing arguments to be made on each of the
  contested issues
- Researching and reviewing the relevant law in your
  case
- Reviewing the facts of your case to determine which
  witnesses are best suited to testify about them
- Reviewing, selecting, and preparing exhibits
- Preparing questions for all witnesses
- Preparing an opening statement
- Preparing a closing argument
- Reviewing rules on evidence to prepare for any
  objections to be made or opposed at trial
- Determining the order of witnesses and all exhibits
- Preparing your file for the day in court, including pre-
  paring a trial notebook with essential information

18.22 How do I know who my witnesses will be at trial?

Well in advance of your trial date, your lawyer will discuss with you whether other witnesses, besides you and your
spouse, will be necessary. Witnesses may include family members, friends, child-care providers, or other people with knowledge relevant to the issues in your case. When thinking of
potential witnesses, consider your relationship with the witness, whether that witness has had an opportunity to observe
relevant facts, and whether the witness has knowledge different from that of other witnesses.

You may also have expert witnesses testify on your behalf.
An expert witness will provide opinion testimony based upon
specialized knowledge, training, or experience. For example, a
psychologist, real estate appraiser, vocational expert, business
valuation expert, or accountant may provide expert testimony
on your behalf.

18.23　Can I prevent my spouse from being in the courtroom?

No, you and your spouse both have a right to be present for hearings and the trial associated with your divorce case.

18.24　Can I take a friend or family member with me to court?

Yes. Let your attorney know in advance if you intend to bring anyone to court with you. Some people close to you may be very emotional about your divorce or your spouse. Be sure to invite someone who is able to provide helpful emotional support for you.

18.25　Can my friends and family be present in the courtroom during my trial?

It depends upon whether they will be witnesses in your case. In most cases in which witnesses other than the husband and wife are testifying, the attorneys request that the judge sequester the witnesses. The judge would then order all witnesses, except you and your spouse, to remain outside the courtroom until it's their turn to testify.

Once a witness has completed his or her testimony, he or she will ordinarily be allowed to remain in the courtroom for the remainder of the trial.

18.26　I want to do a great job testifying in my divorce trial. What are some tips?

Keep the following in mind to be a good witness on your own behalf:

- Tell the truth. Although this may not be always be comfortable, it is critical if you want your testimony to be believed by the judge.
- Listen carefully to the complete question before answering.
- Slow down. It's easy to speed up your speech when you are anxious. Taking your time with your answers ensures that the judge hears you, and that the court reporter can accurately record your testimony.
- If you don't understand a question or don't know the answer, be sure to say so.

- Don't argue with the judge or the lawyers. Be nice and polite. It is important that you be likeable.
- Take your time. You may be asked some questions that call for a thoughtful response. If you need a moment to reflect on an answer before you give it, allow yourself that time.
- Look at your attorney as the questions are being asked, but turn and direct your answer to the judge.
- Speak loudly enough to be easily heard.
- Stop speaking if an objection is made by one of the lawyers. Wait until the judge has decided whether to allow you to answer.

18.27 Should I be worried about being cross-examined by my spouse's lawyer?

If your case goes to trial, prepare to be asked questions by your spouse's lawyer. If you are worried about particular questions, discuss your concerns with your attorney. He can support you in giving a truthful response. Prepare for anticipated questions by your spouse's lawyer. Try not to take the questions personally; remember that the lawyer is fulfilling a duty to advocate for your spouse's interests.

18.28 What should I do if I don't understand a question?

You should say that. The judge will have the attorney repeat the question so you can hear it. If the question is ambiguous or confusing, your attorney can object and the judge will have the other attorney rephrase the question.

18.29 What happens on the day of the trial?

Although no two trials are alike, the following steps will occur in most divorce trials:

- Both attorneys make opening statements discussing the facts and issues in the case, and identifying the evidence they plan to present.
- Plaintiff's attorney calls plaintiff's witnesses to testify. Defendant's attorney may cross-examine each of them.

- Defendant's attorney calls defendant's witness to testify. Plaintiff's attorney may cross-examine each of them.

- Plaintiff's lawyer calls any rebuttal witnesses (these are witnesses whose testimony contradicts the testimony of the defendant's witnesses).

- Closing arguments are made first by the plaintiff's attorney and then by the defendant's attorney.

18.30 Will the judge decide my case the day I go to court?

Possibly, but probably not. Often there is so much information from the trial for the judge to consider that it is not possible for her to give an immediate ruling.

The judge may want to review documents, review the law, perform calculations, review his or her notes, and give thoughtful consideration to the issues to be decided. For this reason, it may be days, weeks, or in some cases even longer before a ruling is made.

When a judge does not make a ruling immediately upon the conclusion of a trial, the case is said to have been "taken under advisement."

18.31 Can I get a different judge?

An attempt to replace the judge is nearly always a waste of time and money. In addition, you should anticipate that the judge will not appreciate the allegations used by your attorney in the attempt. Putting yourself in an explicitly adverse relationship with the judge is not likely to help your case.

19

Appeal

You may find that despite your best efforts to settle your case, it went to trial and the judge made major decisions that will have a serious impact on your future. You may be disappointed or even shocked by the judge's ruling.

The judge might have seen your case differently than you and your attorney did. Perhaps the judge made mistakes. Or it may be that Virginia law simply does not require or even allow for the outcome you were hoping for.

Whatever the reasons for the rulings, you may feel that the judge's decisions are not ones you can live with. If this is the case, talk to your lawyer immediately about your right to appeal. Together you can decide whether an appeal is in your best interests, or whether it is better to accept the court's ruling and invest your energy in moving forward with your future without an appeal.

19.1 How much time after my divorce do I have to file an appeal?

You must file an appeal within thirty days of the final order. Because your attorney may also recommend filing certain motions following your trial, discuss your appeal rights with your lawyer as soon as you have received the judge's ruling. A timely discussion with your attorney about your right to appeal is essential so that important deadlines are not missed.

19.2 Can I appeal a temporary order?

No, only final orders may be appealed.

19.3   How should I decide whether to appeal?

Trial judges have significant discretion on many of the issues in a divorce case, including the grounds of divorce, rulings regarding the assets and debts, spousal support, including the amount and duration, the custody and visitation award, and the award and amount of attorney's fees. What that means is that the judge's rulings will stand unless he made a significant error that affected the outcome of the case.

Though the trial judge has significant discretion, she also has many specific laws and rules that have to be followed that limit that discretion. When analyzing a potential appeal, your attorney has to identify whether the judge made an error by failing to follow or properly apply Virginia law.

You should not appeal simply because you disagree with the judge's rulings. The Virginia Court of Appeals will not reverse the judge if the judge's rulings were within his discretion. To have a chance of success on appeal, you must be able to show that the outcome was wrong because the judge made an error (for example, by misapplying the law, by not following a required procedure, or by making a ruling without supporting evidence).

19.4   What are the odds of winning an appeal?

Most divorce rulings appealed to the Virginia Court of Appeals are upheld by the Court of Appeals. In other words, most appeals fail. Parties often appeal because they are unhappy with the trial judge's ruling, but that is an insufficient basis for an appeal. Realize that it is a rare case in which at least one of the parties is not unhappy with the trial judge's rulings. Don't appeal unless your attorney can identify an actual error committed by the trial judge that affected the outcome, and not just a discretionary ruling with which you disagree.

19.5   What happens if I appeal and win?

This is an important question. In a small percentage of the cases in which a trial judge is overruled, the Court of Appeals makes a substitute ruling and the case is over. In most cases in which a trial judge is overruled, the case is sent back to the trial court, often to the same judge, for a new hearing or trial.

19.6 When should an appeal be filed?

An appeal should be filed only after careful consultation with your lawyer when you believe that the judge has made a serious error under the law or the facts of your case. Among the factors you and your attorney should discuss are:

- Whether the judge had the authority under the law to make the decisions set forth in your divorce order
- The likelihood of the success of your appeal
- The risk that an appeal by you will encourage an appeal by your former spouse
- The cost of the appeal
- The length of time an appeal can be expected to take
- The impact of a delay in the case during the appeal

19.7 Are there any disadvantages to filing an appeal?

There can be disadvantages to filing an appeal, including:

- uncertainty as to the outcome
- attorney's fees and costs
- the risks of a worse outcome on appeal than you received at trial
- delay in finalizing your divorce
- prolonged conflict between you and your former spouse
- risk of a second trial occurring after the appeal
- difficulty in obtaining closure and moving forward with your life

19.8 Is an attorney necessary to appeal?

The appeals process involves detailed and specific court rules and deadlines. Given the complex nature of the appellate process, you should have an attorney if you intend to file an appeal.

19.9 How long does the appeals process usually take?

It depends, though an appeal often takes a year. A successful appeal may also result in the need for further proceedings in the trial court which will result in further delay.

19.10 What are the steps in the appeals process?

There are many steps which your lawyer will take on your behalf in the appeal process, including:

- Identifying the issues to be appealed
- Filing a notice with the court of your intent to appeal
- Obtaining and filing a transcript of trial (a written transcript of the testimony by witnesses, and all statements by the judge and the lawyers made in the presence of the court reporter)
- Performing legal research to support your arguments on appeal
- Preparing and filing a document known as a *brief,* which sets forth the facts of the case and relevant law, complete with citations to the trial transcript, court documents, and prior cases
- Making an oral argument before the judges of the appellate court

19.11 Is filing and pursuing an appeal expensive?

Yes, in addition to filing fees and lawyer fees, there is likely to be a substantial cost for the preparation of the transcript of the trial.

19.12 If I do not file an appeal, can I ever go back to court to change my divorce order?

Certain aspects of an order are not modifiable, such as the division of property and debts and the award of attorney fees. Other parts of your order, such as support or matters regarding the children, may be modified if there has been a material change in circumstances.

A modification of a custody or visitation order would also require you to show that the change would be in the children's best interests.

You should talk to your attorney about what parts of your order are final, and what parts are modifiable.

20

What Happens after the Divorce?

You have finally reached the end of the divorce journey. You may be sad about the end of your marriage, you may be hopeful about the future ahead of you, and you may be worried about different aspects of your new life. These feelings are normal.

It is also normal for you to be unsure about how you take the final actions to complete property transfers, name-change details, and other postdivorce tasks.

Whatever items are on your to-do list, it is best to map out your action plan. Clarify which items are your responsibility and which items will be handled by your attorney.

20.1   What tasks do I have to deal with following the entry of my divorce order?

Some of the tasks you may need to handle include the following:

- Read and comply with the terms of your settlement agreement if your case was settled (for example, re-title cars and real estate).

- Read and comply with the terms of your divorce order (an example would be to transfer interests in retirement accounts).

- Obtain COBRA coverage or new health insurance coverage if you were covered on your spouse's plan

- Clarify with your attorney which postdivorce tasks you will each be responsible for.

151

- Update your estate-planning documents.
- Update your beneficiary information for your life insurance policies and your retirement accounts.

20.2 What do I need to do when the amount of child support changes based on one of my children turning eighteen?

Child support automatically ends when your youngest child turns eighteen and graduates from high school. If you have more than one child, child support does not automatically change when the older children turn eighteen and graduate from high school. In that situation the parents should cooperate in recalculating child support based upon the Virginia guidelines. Have your attorney help, if needed. To be legally enforceable, the new amount needs to be set forth in a new court order.

20.3 What notices do I have to give to the court following my divorce?

Read your court order(s) carefully. Any notice requirements will be set forth in those orders. The most common notice requirement is to give the other party and the court at least thirty day's notice before a move if you have minor children. There may be other notice requirements if there are support obligations.

20.4 My order includes a provision that my former spouse and I both pay a portion of uninsured medical expenses incurred for the minor children. How do I communicate this information, and when do I get reimbursed?

Be sure to provide your former spouse with the required documentation as set forth in your agreement or order. Be sure to keep a copy of all documents you send to the other parent.

Reimbursement of uninsured medical expenses is an issue frequently disputed in support determination and contempt of court proceedings. For this reason, maintain complete records regarding these expenses, such as:

- A copy of all billing statements from the service providers with your notations regarding payments made including the date, amount, and check number

- A copy of all insurance benefits statements
- Monthly or annual printouts of all the charges and payments for prescription drugs from your pharmacy
- A record of sums paid by the other parent, either directly to care providers or reimbursements paid to you
- A copy of correspondence between you and the other parent regarding these expenses

You may want to consider creating a work sheet to help you track expenses and payments. In the event of a future dispute you will then have all of the documentation needed for your attorney to present your case or to defend a claim against you.

20.5 What if my former spouse and I have a disagreement about our custody and visitation arrangements after the divorce order is entered?

Try to work together in a cooperative manner regarding your child. Make every effort to focus on your child's best interests, and avoid a competitive, win-lose relationship with the other parent. If you and the other parent can't resolve the issue, consider involving a child therapist to obtain unbiased input. Involve your attorney, if necessary. Involve the judge as a last resort.

20.6 How do I make my court-ordered payments that are not related to child support or spousal support?

If not otherwise specified, write and send a check to your former spouse with an explanatory note on the memo line. Follow the requirements of your agreement or court order.

20.7 My former spouse has not paid me the property settlement as ordered in the divorce order. What can I do?

In the event that your former spouse does not make court-ordered payments, enforcement mechanisms are available such as contempt of court actions or garnishment. If payment becomes an issue, contact your attorney to discuss your enforcement options.

20.8   I was told by my bank that I need a certified copy of my divorce order. How do I obtain one?

Your divorce order remains permanently on file with the circuit court where your divorce took place. You can obtain a certified copy from the clerk's office for a nominal fee, or your attorney can handle this task for you.

20.9   Is there anything else I should be doing after my divorce?

The following postdivorce checklist covers many actions that may be necessary:

Property

_____ Confirm necessary real estate deeds have been signed and recorded in the appropriate circuit court.

_____ Refinance mortgages as required by your agreement or court order.

_____ Complete the exchange of personal property.

_____ Transfer the title for vehicles.

_____ Transfer or close bank accounts and safe deposit boxes.

_____ Transfer investment accounts, stocks, and bonds.

_____ Review beneficiary designations on retirement and financial accounts for any needed changes.

Property Settlement

_____ Comply with property settlement obligations in a timely manner.

Insurance

_____ Review life insurance beneficiary designation for any needed changes.

_____ Obtain COBRA or other needed health insurance.

_____ Notify employer of divorce.

_____ Make sure your vehicle is insured in your name.

Debts and Liabilities

_____ Cancel joint accounts or charge cards, or remove name of former spouse.

Children

_____ If you are the noncustodial parent, notify child's school of your contact information and your desire to be notified of events and to receive duplicate copy of report cards.

Child Support and Spousal Support

_____ If support is paid directly and not by wage withholding, set up automatic transfers or otherwise arrange for timely payments.

Uninsured Medical Expenses

_____ Set up a tracking and filing system to keep full and complete records regarding these financial matters.

Tax Matters

_____ Notify your employer of the change in your exemption status (complete a new W-4).

_____ If necessary, complete *IRS Form 8822* for change of address.

_____ Arrange to make quarterly payments for taxes due on spousal support.

_____ Refer to *IRS Publication 504, Divorced or Separated Individuals* for other questions.

Attorney Fees

_____ Contact the firm's account manager to make payment arrangements for any fees owed to the firm.

_____ If your former spouse was ordered to pay a portion of your attorney fees, note that you remain responsible for the payment of your attorney fees, including any applicable interest, until the account is paid.

_____ If you have been ordered to pay fees to your former spouse's attorney, make payment pursuant to the divorce order.

Name Change

If your name changed:

_____ Contact the Social Security Administration (SSA) to complete an Application for Social Security Card (Form SS-5). The SSA will notify the IRS of your name change when your new Social Security card is issued.

_____ Notify the division of motor vehicles and your employer regarding your new name.

Estate Planning

_____ Review your will, power of attorney, and advance medical directive for any needed changes.

_____ Schedule an appointment with your attorney to update or prepare your will, power of attorney, advanced medical directive, and other important estate-planning documents.

In Closing

For most people a divorce is definitely a low point in their life. Broken or damaged emotional bonds, financial stress, anger, pain, frustration, unhappiness, depression, and alienation are common. Often things seem so dark that a happy future is impossible to imagine.

The divorce process often takes a year or more. During that time I hope you are able to move beyond many of your most negative emotions and become calmer, less stressed, and less anxious. Seek out people who help you smile, and limit your time with people who seem to focus only on the negative.

Though it seems like a cliché, it is important that you control what you can, and accept what you cannot control. This is important but very difficult. Controlling what you can requires you to focus on the different aspects of your life, and to be disciplined in doing those things that are important. This list includes properly tending to your children, your job, your finances, your relationships, your health, your diet, your exercise, your sleep, etc.

Being focused and disciplined regarding what's important in your life is hard. Accepting what you cannot control may be even harder. In nearly every divorce each spouse is unhappy with the other's attitude and behavior. But your ability to control or steer your spouse's behavior is probably close to nonexistent. This may be difficult to accept, especially if there are children and your dissatisfaction extends to the way your former partner parents your children.

Often it is not clear exactly what you should try to change and what you just need to accept. Your divorce attorney can help you identify which of your spouse's behaviors you have a chance of changing and which behaviors and attitudes you will just have to accept.

I hope you conclude your divorce with the best possible outcome for you and your children and with the least possible contention and expense. All the best to you as your move through this challenging stage in your life.

Appendix

Child Custody and Visitation, Statutory Factors

In determining the best interests of a child for purposes of determining custody or visitation arrangements, the court considers the following:

1. The age and physical and mental condition of the child, giving due consideration to the child's changing developmental needs

2. The age and physical and mental condition of each parent

3. The relationship existing between each parent and each child, giving due consideration to the positive involvement with the child's life, and their ability to accurately assess and meet the emotional, intellectual, and physical needs of the child

4. The needs of the child, giving due consideration to other important relationships of the child, including but not limited to siblings, peers and extended family members

5. The role that each parent has played and will play in the future in the upbringing and care of the child

6. The propensity of each parent to actively support the child's contact and relationship with the other parent, including whether a parent has unreasonably denied the other parent access to or visitation with the child

7. The relative willingness and demonstrated ability of each parent to maintain a close and continuing relationship with the child, and the ability of each parent to cooperate in and resolve disputes regarding matters affecting the child

8. The reasonable preference of the child, if the court deems the child to be of reasonable intelligence, understanding, age and experience to express such a preference

9. Any history of family abuse or sexual abuse. If the court finds such a history, the court may disregard the factors in 6, above.

10. Such other factors as the court deems necessary and proper to the determination

Child-Support Deviation Factors

In making its decision regarding child support, the court will consider the following factors:

1. Actual monetary support for other family members or former family members

2. Arrangements regarding custody of the children, including the cost of visitation travel

3. Imputed income to a party who is voluntarily unemployed or voluntarily underemployed

4. Any child-care costs incurred on behalf of the child or children due to the attendance of a custodial parent in an educational or vocational program likely to maintain or increase the party's earning potential

5. Debts of either party arising during the marriage for the benefit of the child

6. Direct payments ordered by the court for maintaining life insurance coverage, education expenses, or other court-ordered direct payments for the benefit of the child

7. Extraordinary capital gains such as capital gains resulting from the sale of the marital abode

8. Any special needs of a child resulting from any physical, emotional, or medical condition

9. Independent financial resources of the child or children
10. Standard of living for the child or children established during the marriage
11. Earning capacity, obligations, financial resources, and special needs of each parent
12. Provisions made with regard to the marital property where said property earns income or has an income-earning potential
13. Tax consequences to the parties including claims for exemptions, child tax credit, and child-care credit for dependent children
14. A written agreement, stipulation, consent order, or decree between the parties that includes the amount of child support
15. Such other factors as are necessary to consider the equities for the parents and children

Equitable Distribution, Statutory Factors

In making its equitable distribution award, the court shall consider the following factors:

1. The contributions, monetary and nonmonetary, of each party to the well-being of the family
2. The contributions, monetary and nonmonetary, of each party in the acquisition and care and maintenance of such marital property of the parties
3. The duration of the marriage
4. The ages and physical and mental condition of the parties
5. The circumstances and factors that contributed to the dissolution of the marriage, specifically including any ground for divorce
6. How and when specific items of such marital property were acquired
7. The debts and liabilities of each spouse, the basis for such debts and liabilities, and the property that may serve as security for such debts and liabilities

8. The liquid or nonliquid character of all marital property

9. The tax consequences to each party

10. The use or expenditure of marital property by either of the parties for a nonmarital separate purpose or the dissipation of such funds, when such was done in anticipation of divorce or separation or after the last separation of the parties

11. Such other factors as the court deems necessary or appropriate to consider in order to arrive at a fair and equitable monetary award

Spousal Support, Statutory Factors

In making its decision regarding spousal support, the court will consider the following factors:

1. The obligations, needs, and financial resources of the parties, including but not limited to income from all pension, profit-sharing, or retirement plans, of whatever nature

2. The standard of living established during the marriage

3. The duration of the marriage

4. The age and physical and mental condition of the parties and any special circumstances of the family

5. The extent to which the age, physical or mental condition, or special circumstances of any child of the parties would make it appropriate that a party not seek employment outside the home

6. The contributions, monetary and nonmonetary, of each party to the well-being of the family

7. The property interests of the parties, both real and personal, tangible and intangible

8. The provisions made with regard to the marital property

9. The earning capacity, including the skills, education, and training of the parties and the present employment opportunities for persons possessing such earning capacity

Appendix

10. The opportunity for, ability of, and the time and costs involved for a party to acquire the appropriate education, training, and employment to obtain the skills needed to enhance his or her earning ability
11. The decisions regarding employment, career, economics, education, and parenting arrangements made by the parties during the marriage and their effect on present and future earning potential, including the length of time one or both of the parties have been absent from the job market
12. The extent to which either party has contributed to the attainment of education, training, career position, or profession of the other party
13. Such other factors, including the tax consequences to each party, as are necessary to consider the equities between the parties

Resources

Annual Credit Report Request Service
www.annualcreditreport.com
P.O. Box 105283
Atlanta, GA 30348-5283
Phone: (877) 322-8228
This website offers a centralized service for consumers to request annual credit reports. It was created by the three nationwide consumer credit reporting companies, Equifax, Experian, and TransUnion. AnnualCreditReport.com processes requests for free credit file disclosures (commonly called credit reports). Under the Fair and Accurate Credit Transactions Act (FACT Act), consumers can request and obtain a free credit report once every twelve months from each of the three nationwide consumer credit reporting companies. AnnualCreditReport.com offers consumers a fast and convenient way to request, view, and print their credit reports in a secure Internet environment. It also provides options to request reports by telephone and by mail.

Child Support Calculator
www.divorcehq.com/cgi-support/calcentry.pl?id=50517 &state=Virginia

Circuit Court Forms
www.courts.state.va.us/forms/circuit/home.html
This website provides forms for Virginia circuit courts.

Division of Child Support Enforcement (DCSE)
www.dss.virginia.gov/family/dcse/index.cgi
Phone: (800) 468-8894
The Child Support Enforcement Program helps parents collect child support. Use the website to find your district office or e-mail about any child-support subject.

Divorce Law
www.vadivorcelaw.net
Raynor Law Office
211 5th St., NE
Charlottesville, VA 22902
Phone: (434) 220-6066
This website is managed by the author's law office. It provides information regarding Virginia law governing divorce and other family law topics.

Internal Revenue Service (IRS)
www.irs.gov
Phone: (800) 829-1040 for assistance with individual tax questions or (800) 829-4933 for assistance with business tax questions.

The IRS website allows you to search using key words, review publications and information on tax questions, or submit a question via e-mail or telephone to an IRS representative.

Juvenile and Domestic Relations Forms
www.courts.state.va.us/forms/district/jdr.html
This website provides forms for juvenile and domestic relations courts.

Legal Aid
www.valegalaid.org
Phone: (866) 534-5243 for eligibility.
This website provides links for self-help forms, information regarding divorce issues, locations of legal aid offices, court information, and links to finding legal help.

Raynor Law Office
www.vadivorcelaw.net
211 5th St., NE
Charlottesville, VA 22902
This is the website of the author's law office. The website provides additional divorce information and resources, including a tool to calculate child support.

Social Security Administration (SSA)
www.ssa.gov
Office of Public Inquiries
Windsor Park Building
1100 West High Rise
Baltimore, MD 21235
Phone: (800) 772-1213
The website enables users to search by question or word, submit questions via e-mail, and review recent publications.

Virginia State Bar
www.vimeo.com/16997474
"Spare the Child" video, approximately eighteen minutes long, is recommended for divorcing parents with minor children.

Virginia Supreme Court Forms
www.courts.state.va.us/forms
This website provides forms for Virginia courts.

Glossary

Collaborative divorce: A specific process of working together to reach a mutually acceptable outcome regarding the various divorce issues. Both parties hire attorneys trained in the collaborative practice process, and the parties and the attorneys all sign a contract committing to the process, agreeing to full disclosure, and stipulating that the attorneys will not participate in litigation in the event all issues are not resolved collaboratively.

Court, Appeals: The Virginia Court of Appeals has jurisdiction of family law appeals from the circuit courts.

Court, Circuit: Each locality in Virginia has a circuit court. The circuit courts in Virginia have jurisdiction to handle divorce cases, including all related issues. The circuit courts also have jurisdiction of appeals from the juvenile courts.

Court, Juvenile: Each locality in Virginia has a juvenile and domestic relations district court. Though the juvenile courts do not have jurisdiction to handle divorce cases, they do have jurisdiction to handle custody and visitation, spousal support and child support, plus certain other family law disputes.

Defendant: The spouse not filing the divorce complaint

Discovery: The voluntary exchange of information can be done at any stage of the proceedings. Once a lawsuit is filed, both parties are allowed to engage in discovery as stated in the Virginia rules of court. Discovery includes interrogatories (written questions to be answered by the other party under oath), requests for production of documents, requests for admission, depositions (oral questioning of a party or a witness under oath, before a court reporter), and subpoenas *duces tecum* (requests to non-parties for documents).

Guardian *ad litem*: When custody or visitation is an issue, either in a divorce case in circuit court, or as a result of a petition in juvenile and domestic relations district court, the judge may appoint an attorney to represent the children. The attorney appointed to represent the children is a guardian *ad litem*. His or her role is to represent the children in the court proceeding.

Litigation: The legal process and procedures involved in a court action, leading up to and including the hearing or trial.

Material change in circumstances: A significant, unforeseen change in relevant facts that allows the judge to reconsider spousal support, custody, visitation, or child-support rulings. (Note: the judge cannot modify agreed-upon spousal support unless the agreement allows modification.)

Mediation: A process or means of resolving differences by agreement. The parties meet with one or two mediators, discuss the issues in dispute, and explore ways of trying to resolve the differences. Mediators do not rule on the dispute. Instead, they are trained to help the parties themselves work out a mutually acceptable solution. Some mediators are attorneys or retired judges. The attorneys for the parties may, but are not required to, attend mediation sessions.

Parties: In divorce cases the parties are the spouses, referred to specifically as the *plaintiff* and the *defendant*.

Pendente lite: Once a complaint is filed initiating a divorce action, either party can request temporary, or *pendente lite* ("pending the suit"), relief. The court may hold a hearing and enter an order regarding spousal support, child custody, visitation, child support, exclusive use and possession of the marital residence, and restrictions on the transfer or use of assets. This relief lasts until there is a final order in the case which supersedes the prior order of temporary relief.

Plaintiff: The spouse filing the divorce complaint

Pleading: A document in which the allegations or responses of parties to a lawsuit are presented in proper form; specifically the complaint of a plaintiff and the answer of a defendant plus any additional papers (such as motions and notices) that are authorized by law.

Index

171

Index

Index

hidden assets, 64, 68
hourly rates as attorney's fees, 24
household goods, 63–64
house/home, 61–64
    during divorce process, possession of, 35–37
    payments on, 41
    taxes on, 110
hybrid assets, 61
hybrid property, 61

I

illegal tracking, 40–41
impute income, 83
income, 99
    impute, 83
    spousal support and, 81, 83
    taxes, 107–108
information. *see also* documentation
    during depositions, 133
    disclosure of all, to attorney, 13, 43
    discovery process, requests for, 130
    on emergency, 51–52
    financial, 5
    gathering of, coping with, 45
    for initial consultation, 9–10
    responding to requests for, 31
    spousal support, provided for receiving, 80
    writing, 30
inheritances, 66
initial consultation, 9–12, 23
innocent spouse relief, 112
insurance
    health, 76–78, 103
    life, 74–75
interest on past-due child support, 104
interrogatories, 128, 130–132. *see also* discovery process

interviewing attorney, 8
IRA, 73, 111
IRS Form 8332, 111
IRS Form W-4, Employee's Withholding Certificate, 111
IRS Publication 504, Divorced or Separated Individuals, 109
IRS Publication 523, Selling Your Home, 110
IRS Publication 529, Miscellaneous Deductions, 111
IRS Publication 971, Innocent Spouse Relief, 111

J

joint accounts, 38–39
joint income tax return, 109
joint legal child custody, 86
judge
    assets division and, 67
    child/children, speaking with, 88
    child custody and, 86
    child support and, 104
    court and, 146
    property division and, 67
    property settlement agreement, approval of, 69
    selection of, 146
    settlement agreement, approval of, 123
jurisdiction, 10
jury, 137

K

kidnapping, 54

L

late child support, 106
law of language, 10
lawyer. *see* attorney
Legal Aid, 31–32
legal assistant, 15–16
legal child custody, 86, 92
legal fees. *see* fees

177

Index

relocation and, 57
service, 10
serving divorce papers to
spouse, 59, 125
serving of complaint for divorce,
125
settlement agreement. *see
also* property settlement
agreement
court and, 120, 139
divorce order and, 127
divorce process and, 2
forcing other parties response
to, 19
judge's approval of, 123
modifying, 122
for property, division of, 69
remaining open to, 31
steps following approval of,
123
trial and, 29, 123
written, 120
settlement conference, 116–
123. *see also* mediation;
negotiations
alternatives to, 120
facilitating, 18
fees for, 116–117
negotiations prior to, 117–
118
options for, 119
partial agreements during,
122
preparing for, 121–122
spouse, attendance to, 48
trial and, 120
sexual orientation, 90
shared physical child custody,
91
significant other, 83, 102
smartphones, 41
social media, 12
Social Security, 74
sole child custody, 91–92

sole legal child custody, 86
split child custody, 92
spousal support, 79–84
accuracy of record of, 82
affair and, 82
bankruptcy and, 84
calculating, 79–80
death and, 82
duration of marriage and, 83
eligibility for, 79
failure to pay, 83–84
formula for deterring, 80
income and, 81, 83
information provided for
receiving, 80
length of time for receiving,
80
material change in
circumstance for, 81
modifying, 81
out-of-state relocation and,
82
payments for, 20, 80
permanent, 80
purpose of, 81
reducing, 81
remarriage and, 82
request following finality of
divorce, 84
reservation of, 84
retirement and, 84
significant other and, 83
statutory factors for, 162–163
taxes on, 82, 108
unemployment and, 83
spouse
aggressive behavior of, 37
agreement for divorce, 2
amicable divorce with, 5
anger towards, 48
arguing with, 93
attorney's fees, responsibility
for paying, 34
communications with, 40,

Index

truth, 47
Twitter, 12
U
under oath, 128
unemployment, 83
Uniform Child Custody
  Jurisdiction and Enforcement
  Act (UCCJEA), 55
uninsured medical expenses,
  20–21
  action plan following divorce
  for, 152–153
  child support and, 103
United States Constitution, 133
V
valuation of property, 67
vehicles, 64
video to help judge determine
  child custody, 91
Virginia Court of Appeals, 148
Virginia Division of Child
  Support Enforcement (DCSE),
  33, 100–101, 104–105
visitation, 85–96. *see also* child
  custody
  action plan following divorce
  for, 153
  arrangements for, 18

child support and, 98
compromise settlement of,
  87
defined, 86
guardian *ad litem,* role of,
  87–88
refusal for, 39, 93
returning child from, 89, 93
schedule for, 87
statutory factors for, 159–160
vocational experts, 14
voluntarily paying child support,
  100
W
wage withholding order, 106
waiting period for divorce, 59
website for attorney, 30
withdrawal of attorney for
  nonpayment of attorney's
  fees, 34
witnesses, 90, 134, 143
writing information, 30
written fee agreement, 25
written settlement agreement,
  120
Y
Yahoo, 12

About the Author

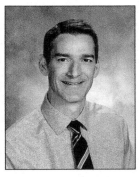

Steven L. Raynor is an attorney in private practice in Charlottesville, Virginia. He graduated from Randolph-Macon College with a BA in philosophy, and from the University of Virginia School of Law with a J.D. degree. Since 1990, Mr. Raynor's practice has focused on family law. He has handled hundreds of cases with a high percentage of settlements. He has handled cases ranging from child custody and child support to complicated cases involving tens of millions of dollars. He has litigated cases ranging from short hearings to a month long trial.

Mr. Raynor is a member of the Family Law Section of the American Bar Association, a member of the Board of Governors of the Family Law Section of the Virginia State Bar, a council member of the Domestic Relations Section of the Virginia Bar Association, and the chair of the Family, Juvenile and Domestic Relations Section of the Charlottesville—Albemarle Bar Association.

He has contributed to attorney education in the family law practice area through continuing legal education seminar presentations, professional articles, and his firm's website, www.vadivorcelaw.net.

Mr. Raynor has been listed by the *Virginia Business* magazine as one of the legal elite in the family/domestic relations practice area, he has been selected to the Virginia Super Lawyers list in the family law practice area, and he has been identified as one of the Top Ten Family Law Attorneys in Virginia by the National Academy of Family Law Attorneys.

Mr. Raynor may be reached through his website: **www.raynorlawoffice.com.**

Divorce Titles from Addicus Books
Visit our online catalog at www.AddicusBooks.com

Divorce in Alabama: The Legal Process, Your Rights, and What to Expect $21.95

Divorce in Arizona: The Legal Process, Your Rights, and What to Expect. $21.95

Divorce in California: The Legal Process, Your Rights, and What to Expect $21.95

Divorce in Connecticut: The Legal Process, Your Rights, and What to Expect $21.95

Divorce in Georgia: The Legal Process, Your Rights, and What to Expect $21.95

Divorce in Hawaii: The Legal Process, Your Rights, and What to Expect $21.95

Divorce in Illinois: The Legal Process, Your Rights, and What to Expect $21.95

Divorce in Louisiana: The Legal Process, Your Rights, and What to Expect $21.95

Divorce in Maine: The Legal Process, Your Rights, and What to Expect $21.95

Divorce in Michigan: The Legal Process, Your Rights, and What to Expect. $21.95

Divorce in Mississippi: The Legal Process, Your Rights, and What to Expect. $21.95

Divorce in Missouri: The Legal Process, Your Rights, and What to Expect $21.95

Divorce in Nebraska: The Legal Process, Your Rights, and What to Expect—2nd Edition $21.95

Divorce in Nevada: The Legal Process, Your Rights, and What to Expect. $21.95

Divorce in New Jersey: The Legal Process, Your Rights, and What to Expect $21.95

Divorce in New York: The Legal Process, Your Rights, and What to Expect $21.95

Divorce in Tennessee: The Legal Process, Your Rights, and What to Expect $21.95

Divorce in Texas: The Legal Process, Your Rights, and What to Expect $21.95

Divorce in Virginia: The Legal Process, Your Rights, and What to Expect $21.95

Divorce in Washington: The Legal Process, Your Rights, and What to Expect $21.95

Divorce in West Virginia: The Legal Process, Your Rights, and What to Expect $21.95

Divorce in Wisconsin: The Legal Process, Your Rights, and What to Expect $21.95

To Order Books:
Visit us online at: www.AddicusBooks.com
Call toll free: (800) 888-4741

 Addicus Books
P. O. Box 45327
Omaha, NE 68145

*Addicus Books is dedicated to publishing books
that comfort and educate.*

Made in the USA
Middletown, DE
08 March 2023

26403765R00109